To Ch[...] lease A tr[...] Pro! Dave

THE LITTLE BOOK OF

TRIPLE NET LEASE

INVESTING

Jonathan W. Hipp
& David Sobelman

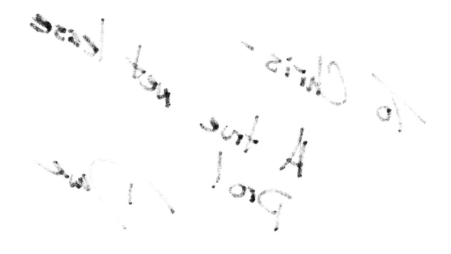

Table of Contents

Foreword

Welcome to the only book you'll ever need to read about triple net lease investments. And while we may be in the business of selling such investments, we assure that our fiduciary responsibility to our clients comes first. Because of this, our book presents objective information about "triple nets" and the brokerage firms that handle these investments. We'll lay out the advantages and disadvantages involved with these topics, thus allowing you to make the best financial choice in any given situation regarding the investments that you're considering.

At this point, you may be wondering, "Why is this book necessary?" Well, on the surface, triple net lease investments are simple. But dig a little deeper and you'll find that the process can be quite complicated and that there are many different avenues to consider. It's definitely no place for amateurs. A lot of money and obligations are at stake, which is why most investors need a professional brokerage firm to help them safely navigate the legal minefields.

The content in this book is the culmination of our firm's more than 20 years of experience in the field. During that time we've successfully handled transactions ranging from $1 million to over $50 million. We know the ins and outs of the business, and we'd like to share that insider knowledge with you.

By the time you're done reading, you'll be ready to enter into the triple net lease transaction field and enjoy the benefits of lower-risk income, preservation of capital and many, many other advantages. Enjoy the journey!

An Introduction to Triple Net Lease Investments

Welcome to the wonderful world of triple net lease investments (also called "NNNs" or "triple nets"). Yes, we know that the term "wonderful" may sound a bit over the top, but frankly most people find the subject to be pretty boring. That is, until they start getting income from these investments. Suddenly, the concept becomes wonderful!

Because triple nets can be such a vital part of your financial future, we feel you should understand them as completely possible. That's why we've written this book. We want to give you a clear and complete understanding of triple nets so that, as a real estate investor, you can make informed decisions on such investments.

The Basic Definition

We'll get into the specifics of triple nets and their variations throughout this book, but for now it's just important for you to know the basic definition of an NNN, which is: a net lease where a building tenant agrees to pay a monthly lump sum base rent as well as the:

- Property taxes
- Property insurance
- Maintenance costs

There are several advantages to triple net leases, which are considered one of the more secure investments you can put your hard-earned money into. Here they are:

Benefit 1: Lower-Risk Income

As an investor, you're well aware that the financial markets inevitably fluctuate depending on the economy and other factors beyond your control. Your goal as an investor is to "flatten out" that rollercoaster ride by putting your money into stable investments that generate income even during the "low points" of those fluctuations.

Many investors consider single-tenant, net-leased properties to be a good choice in any environment because of these investments' bond-like quality. Like bonds, single-tenant, net-leased properties provide steady and predictable returns over time.

But wait, there's more. Because tenants commit to long-term leases, there's also lower re-leasing risk. Finally, you can tailor these investments to your risk-reward expectations by choosing tenants with different credit profiles. For example, some tenants are rated by national credit-rating agencies while other tenants have only their previous financial performance as recommendations. You can pick and choose among these investments.

Benefit 2: Preservation of Capital

As mentioned above, the financial markets are sometimes unpredictable, with many investors suffering major losses at times. With triple net lease investments, you can avoid this money-losing scenario and keep your capital intact through all the uncertainty.

Benefit 3: Tax Deferment

This is a really great benefit. Via a 1031 or 1033 exchange, you can defer 100 percent of the capital gains tax from the sale of your net lease property. We'll go in-depth about this subject later in the book because it should be an integral part of your overall financial strategy.

Benefit 4: Relief from Management Obligations

Many of our property-owning investors love this benefit the best. With no management obligations, they don't have the constant hassle that comes with managing a property – time, money, maintenance worries, tenant management, and so forth. With a triple net lease investment, all these burdens are off your shoulders.

Benefit 5: Providing Estate Assets for Your Heirs

Triple net lease investments can be the "gifts that keep on giving." With proper estate planning, you can pass them (and the income generated by them) onto your heirs upon your death. In fact, these investments have the potential to generate income for your heirs for years to come. One method of doing this is via the establishment of a living trust. We are not in the trust business, but we recommend that you investigate this subject further with a reputable professional.

Benefit 6: Flexibility

At this point, you may be thinking, "Will triple nets be adaptable enough to fit my specific needs?" While we obviously don't know your specific needs, we can tell you that these investments are highly flexible. They can meet the financial goals of an individual like yourself, as well as those of partnerships, large institutional investors like real estate investment trusts, life insurance companies, and pension funds.

Benefit 7: Pride of Ownership

This is a pretty subjective benefit, but it's one that investors love most. That's because many of them feel a great sense of pride in the properties they own through triple net lease investments. They can watch them blossom and grow like very profitable financial flowers.

Assessing the Risks

Now we'd next like to acquaint you with the risks of triple net lease investments. This is important because investors sometimes make the mistake of thinking that triple nets are risk-free. Sure these investments are secure overall, but they do have risks (albeit extremely low in relation to other investments). Here are some of the issues to watch out for:

Risk 1: The Lease Itself

Triple net leases themselves are complicated documents that must be properly read and understood from the outset. Ignore this step and you'll wind up with a lease comprised of unexpected expenses, cancellation clauses, and/or default penalties that have no teeth. If you enter into a triple net unprepared, you risk having a "financial leg" blown off. These complex leases require the services of brokers, attorneys, and other experts. See Appendix A for an example of a typical triple net lease.

Risk 2: Credit Worthiness

In the case of triple nets, the creditworthiness of the tenant is of utmost concern, and serves as a vital measure of the risk involved. With triple net lease investments, risk is reflected in the company's credit rating. For example, using the credit rating agencies (Standard and Poor's, Moody's, etc.), those public companies with a rating of BBB- and higher (S&P scale) are considered "investment grade."

In the case of private companies, the investment team will require financial statements in order to evaluate the credit worthiness of individual firms.

Risk 3: Reusability of a Property

With triple net investments, you must consider the reusability of a property, should the tenant vacate the building. A vacancy can be caused by a number of factors – expiration of the lease, tenant default, bankruptcy, economic downturns, etc.

When a vacancy occurs, you lose income at least until another tenant is placed in the property. Your investment managers should be aware of the tenant's financial situation well before that exodus occurs. For example, if the term of the lease is due to expire soon, or if the tenant becomes slow in paying (a "red flag" that would be noticed by your investment team), your team should pick up on it and be ready to act.

When these situations occur, the investment managers could default the tenant and cancel the lease. They could then re-lease the property to a new, creditworthy tenant and charge an equal or higher rate. Another option is to sell the property for a profit and reinvest the gain in other real estate.

Weighing the Options

Now you know the rewards and risks of triple net lease investments. The remainder of this book provides you with an in-depth exploration of all aspects of these investments. This information will enable you to make the most objective decisions possible on the suitability of net lease investments in order to help you achieve your financial goals. As we said earlier, enjoy the journey!

Understanding the Various Types of Net Lease Investments

By this point in the book, you may have wondered where the term "net" lease comes from. Put simply, it's a means of distinguishing such leases from "gross" leases in real estate. Here's the difference between the two:

- With a gross lease, the tenant pays a gross amount of rent. From that rent, the landlord can pay expenses, or spend it in any other way that he or she wants to.
- With a net lease, the property owner receives the rent "net" after all the expenses are passed through to tenants.

In commercial real estate, net leases are a matter of negotiation between the tenant and the property owner. These negotiations typically revolve around expenses like maintenance, repairs, utilities, insurance, real estate taxes, and so forth.

As a result of these negotiations, there are a variety of lease forms to fit the needs of both property owners and tenants. In this chapter we'll explain the most common types, and provide you with a good base of knowledge upon which to make investment decisions.

NNN ("Triple Net") Lease

As described earlier in this chapter, the triple net lease is a net lease where the tenant agrees to pay a monthly lump sum base rent as well as the property taxes, the property insurance, and the maintenance. It's also known as a "bond lease" or "absolute triple net lease."

NN Lease

This is a net lease where the tenant agrees to pay a monthly lump sum base rent, plus the property taxes and insurance. The landlord may be responsible for the maintenance of the roof, the structure of the building, and, perhaps, the parking lot, while the tenant is responsible for all other operating expenses of the premises. Of course, there are many variations of this type of lease but the essence is that the landlord will ultimately have some responsibilities, albeit not day-to-day, for the building.

Modified Net Lease

This is a compromise between the gross lease and the triple net. Usually, the landlord and tenant agree to split the maintenance expenses, while the tenant agrees to pay taxes and insurance. Utilities are often also negotiated in the modified net lease.

Modified Gross Lease

With this form of lease, the landlord generally pays for the base yearly property taxes and building insurance. In general, tenants are responsible for their share of common area operating expenses and common area utilities.

Which Choice is Best?

From an investor's point of view, the triple net lease is most likely the best choice. It tends to be the norm for the industry and is highly sought after for the benefits described in the previous chapter, namely: no property management responsibilities, lower-risk income, tax deferrals, etc.

As an added bonus, many single-tenant triple net lease properties are guaranteed by high profile, profitable corporate tenants like Wendy's, CVS, Blockbuster and Subway.

In the next chapter, we'll look at the typical property categories for triple net lease investments.

Typical Property Categories for Triple Net Lease Investments

Before we start defining property categories, we want you to understand the general forms of ownership and leasing within those categories. There are three of them:

Fee Simple

"Fee simple" is ownership of both land and building. The law recognizes it as the "highest form" of real estate ownership. If you're the property owner, you're entitled to full enjoyment of the property, limited only by zoning laws, deed or subdivision restrictions or covenants.

Unlike a lease, the duration of your ownership is not limited. That means you can pass it along in a will to your heirs. Other terms for fee simple are "fee ownership" and "estate of inheritance."

Ground (Land) Lease

Essentially, a ground lease means that the investor/landlord owns the land only. He or she can then lease out this area for building construction. For example, if you were the owner of a parcel of land, you could lease it out to, say, a corporate client like Walgreens, or a private client wishing to construct a commercial building upon the site.

In its most fundamental form, a ground lease separates land ownership from the ownership of the improvements on the land, such as a shopping center, office building, etc.

Most ground leases are long-term, and typically include:

- Set rent escalations.
- Foreclosure rights should the lessee default.

- A reversionary right (i.e., improvements on the property revert to the landowner at the end of the lease term).

Ground leases can be subordinated or unsubordinated. A subordinated lease is used mainly for long-term ownership projects. Essentially, it's a profit-sharing agreement. As an investor, you participate in the venture's profits above the lease payment. Ideally, those profits steadily mount as rent normally increases over the years, and as the property appreciates.

Unsubordinated ground leases refer to situations when the owner owns the land only and the tenant(s) construct a building on that land at their own cost. These leases are popular for several reasons: there's no building ownership, and the landlord is guaranteed not to be responsible for any maintenance at any time (because he or she doesn't own the building).

Additionally, the building ownership with unsubordinated ground leases usually reverts to the ground landlord. That's because after the tenants leave the building, they don't take that building with them. The landlord gets a free building on the ground that he or she purchased.

If you're a patient investor, unsubordinated leases offer several investment possibilities in that they can be traded, sold, and/or transferred in some creative financial ways. In some situations, for example, you can employ a tax-deferred 1031 strategy. Plus, in some municipal ground lease opportunities, property taxes may be nearly or completely eliminated. Finally, the value can increase when the zoning for land is changed to permit more intensive use of that property.

There are other benefits to unsubordinated leases. You'll want to talk to a knowledgeable triple net expert about such benefits. See Appendix B for an example of a ground lease.

Leasehold

In the commercial real estate sector, leasehold refers to the right to hold or use a building for a fixed period of time at an agreed-upon price without transfer of ownership. In other words, leasehold refers to the structure only, not the land upon which it's built. The lease agreement spells out the rights and obligations of both the landlord or property owner and the tenant. You'll recall that this is the opposite of a ground lease.

Below, we've provided two case studies to illustrate the difference between a ground lease situation and a leasehold opportunity and to show how these types of leases can benefit everyone involved.

Case Study 1 – Ground Lease

In this situation, a developer buys a large tract of land, divides it into parcels for smaller tenants; ground leases them, and then sells them.

One of our clients, "Mr. Smith," had the opportunity to buy a large tract of land. Historically, it had been used as a cattle ranch, but it lay in the "path of progress;" that is, it was obvious that future development was headed in this tract's direction. The 25-acre site was too big for any one tenant for this particular location, but Mr. Smith thought that a new grocery store would do well there. The decision was made to build a shopping center with the grocery store as the large anchor tenant.

The project took up about 10 acres, leaving about 10 acres of developable land, minus five acres for water retention, road setbacks, access to the site, and so forth.

Mr. Smith then subdivided the remaining 10 acres into six parcels of roughly 1.5 acres each. These parcels were located in front of the grocery store along the main road. (In real estate vocabulary, they're called "outparcels.") This term refers to building lots separated or separable from a commercial development. In this case, it was the grocery-anchored shopping center.

Then, Mr. Smith found tenants for each of these smaller tracts and signed ground leases with each tenant of 15 years or 20 years. Tenants included banks, restaurants, auto parts stores, and other retailers.

Now, Mr. Smith had just put out a large capital expenditure by buying 25 acres and then building a grocery store. By doing ground leases for the various outparcels, he could get income from the land without having to spend money to construct a building.

In effect, Mr. Smith owns a grocery store and six outparcels generating income from tenants who wanted to be in front of a high-traffic grocery store.

Now that he has the tenants and income in place, Mr. Smith can decide if he wants to sell those outparcels to a passive triple net investor. He's done all of the work to stabilize the property, and has successfully made it a passive, income-producing asset.

Case Study 2 – Ground Lease

Here's another example of a ground lease, this time from the landowner's point of view:

Ms. Jones is a citrus grower who owns a large tract of land that's been in her family for 100 years. Since her grandfather purchased the land, it's been a strong part of her family legacy and has sentimental value. Ms. Jones doesn't want to sell the land because she'd like to pass it down to her children as the previous generations have done.

But the farming business isn't what it used to be, and she'd like to generate income for her family while retaining ownership of the land. Through a commercial broker, Ms. Jones learns that Home Depot is willing to lease the ground for a 20-year period with the option to extend the term another 20 years in five-year increments. With this deal, Home Depot will control the land for 40 years.

When the lease is signed, Ms. Jones has a potential income stream for 40 years, and Home Depot doesn't have to need an initial capital outlay to purchase the land.

At the end of the lease term, when Home Depot vacates, Ms. Jones will attain possession of the land once again. In this case, the ground lease solution solidly meets the needs of both parties.

Case Study 3 – Leasehold

Okay, now let's study exactly the same example as described above for Mr. Smith, only this time we'll look at it from a tenant's leasehold point of view rather than Mr. Smith's ground lease perspective. This will help you understand the investor benefits of such arrangements.

The same tenants mentioned above for Mr. Smith's buildings (banks, auto parts stores, etc.), construct their facilities on the ground-leased land. While they do not own the land, they own the improvements they put on the land (these are known as leasehold improvements). This is still a real estate deal, but there's no land involved. If the tenants want to sell the improvements, those improvements can only be purchased separately from the land. In this case, the owner has a depreciable asset, but it's subject to the lease terms of the ground lease.

Let's use an example to illustrate this situation. We'll assume that Bank of America puts up a building on one of Mr. Smith's outparcels. However, since the bank doesn't own the land, it decides to sell the leasehold improvements to an investor. That investor can now purchase the leasehold and get income from the property for the term of the lease. In most cases, this is 20 years.

So, what happens if and when Bank of America decides to vacate the building? The leasehold owner can find another tenant for the building and pay the ground rent for that site. Or, he or she can potentially take a capital loss since control of the leasehold will be lost to the ground owner (check with an accountant for further details on capital loss).

Developers and tenants who want to construct build-to-suit developments for specific tenants can sell the improvements – typically at a higher cap rate – because there's no long-term control of the ground. Additionally, the price and risk can be lower because there's no ground to purchase from the outset, which means a lower initial cost.

Real Estate Categories

Now let's look at the real estate categories in which you can invest in the form of triple net leases. Generally speaking, the most common categories available for triple net leases are retail, office and industrial. However, many other categories can be sold on a triple net lease basis, including multifamily, hotel properties, service centers, undeveloped land, health care facilities, and educational buildings, among others.

Office Buildings

As the name suggests, these buildings are built to provide offices for businesses of all types. The attractiveness of such buildings depends upon a number of factors, including available space, design, leasing terms, location and so forth. Office buildings attract clients based on their design and available space.

For your reference, office buildings have an A through D classification in real estate to indicate their quality and desirability. Here are the specific descriptions of each classification:

Office Building Classifications

- *Class A Building* — the highest quality, newer, larger buildings with state-of-the-art amenities such as telecommunication/Internet capabilities. These buildings are located in desirable areas, and typically meet the needs of tenants who require higher-end finishes and amenities. In some cases, tenants also require security, LEED certification, and other features needed by restaurants, health clubs, etc. From an investor's point of view, a Class A building also shows long-term investment benefits.

- *Class B Building* — typically, an average building that may be more than 10 years old with many amenities and located in a desirable area.
- *Class C Building* — typically, a below-average building. Such properties may be older, well-maintained buildings but contain smaller size units. Class C buildings are commonly located in areas where lease rates are stable.
- *Class D Building* — older buildings with high vacancy rates, lack of maintenance, and few amenities. They are often located in or near marginal areas.

Retail

The retail category is broad, and includes the following types of businesses:

Banks

Bank properties are a good choice for triple net lease investment because they're solid tenants, for the most part. The institutions build their reputations on security and longevity and are likely to be good long-term tenants of any properties they occupy. Additionally, transparency is high for banks due to FDIC regulations and public disclosures.

Discount "Big Box" Stores

The term "big box" refers to the powerful discount chains such as Wal-Mart, Target and Costco. Their nickname comes from their large size, which ranges anywhere from 200,000 square feet to over 1 million square feet.

Drug Stores

Drug stores and, in particular, chains like Walgreens, CVS and Rite-Aid, make good triple net lease tenants. That's because customers need medicine no matter what the economic climate. There are several other reasons why drug stores are great triple net investments, including:

- The U.S. population continues to grow; therefore, more people will need medicine.
- Thanks to modern science, people are living longer, and senior citizens require more medication than younger individuals.
- Also thanks to modern science, more new drugs than ever are being introduced into the market place. Often, these drugs are extremely expensive.
- Many new products (stocked by drug stores) have been produced to meet the needs of customers – painkillers, electric toothbrushes, vitamins, contact lens solutions, etc.
- "Impulse" items (candy, cosmetics, greeting cards, etc.) are all available in drug stores. It's been reported that these medicine-centered businesses get from 30 to 35% of their total sales from such non-pharmaceutical products.

Restaurants

This is a popular category for commercial property investments because:

- The vast majority of restaurants operate under an absolute triple net lease.
- Everyone has to eat, especially with so many two wage-earner families these days. As of 2009, the National Restaurant Association was reporting sales of $566 Billion from 945,000 locations with a total of 13 million employees. (Source: http://www.restaurant.org/research/ind_glance.cfm)
- By their very nature, restaurant facilities are well kept and maintained. Nobody wants to eat at dirty or unattractive facilities, plus restaurants must meet state health standards in order to keep operating.
- Typically, restaurants have to be in high-traffic, high-visibility locations in order to attract the traffic they need.

Corporate-owned, national brand restaurants are considered a much safer investment than an individually owned franchise or an independent operation. Corporate ownership usually means less risk because of the sheer financial credit and "might" of the particular company as compared to smaller operations.

24

Plus, there's the power of name recognition. When McDonalds opens its doors, customers will be at those doors, thanks to brand recognition. With a 47 percent market share (as of this writing), McDonalds is the proverbial 800-pound gorilla in the fast food sector. Burger King follows up with a 15 percent market share. So, as an investor, you have the security of knowing the likelihood of long-term success with a national restaurant operation is very high.

Industrial/Manufacturing

The industrial/manufacturing sector comprises a wide variety of businesses. These firms can be divided into the traditional "dirty" businesses (chemicals, petroleum, steel, etc.), and the modern "clean" industries (computers, electronics, etc.). Often, these properties are concentrated in business and industrial "parks."

Many times, you find the "clean" industries concentrated in business parks, and such parks may include distribution centers, medical manufacturing, electronic manufacturing and so forth. Industrial parks hold the dirty industries (traditional manufacturers and distribution centers).

In terms of overall value, business parks tend to have higher value than industrial parks since they attract service businesses (banks, restaurants, and so forth) to serve the greater population of office workers. In other words, they have more multiuse capabilities than the industrial parks, where businesses are targeted to the manufacture of specific products. Business parks tend to incur a lower risk of vacancy and, thus, create a greater assurance of uninterrupted revenue.

Overall, industrial buildings have a variety of classifications, including warehouse, manufacturing, research, and development space. They may range in size from 10,000 square feet to 500,000 square feet, and come with or without attached office space. In keeping with new storage technology, modern warehouses can be more highly specialized than older structures.

Manufacturing facilities usually contain the largest number of special-purpose features, including overhead cranes, reinforced concrete floors, drainage wells, and special lighting and exhaust systems. Such designs can preclude the use of these building by other businesses. Plus, there's always the possible presence of hazardous materials, which can incur expensive liability in the event of spills, explosions, and other accidents.

Okay, now that we've provided an overview of the typical property categories for triple net lease investments, it's time to see how the properties within those categories are valued. That's the subject of the next chapter.

How Triple Net Lease Properties Are Valued

Triple net lease properties should be evaluated with a somewhat conservative approach since most investors are seeking passive income. Here are the four steps that all investors should take:

Step 1: Evaluate the real estate itself.

Step 2: Evaluate the creditworthiness of the tenant.

Step 3: Evaluate the lease.

Step 4: Compare and analyze the information from steps 1-3 in order to generate a capitalization rate and a decision regarding the property.

Before we walk you through these four steps, you'll need to understand the concept of a capitalization rate or "cap rate." (The triple net lease market is driven by this calculation.) The cap rate is the ratio between the net operating income produced by an asset and its capital cost (the original price paid to buy the asset) or by its current market value. The rate is calculated in a simple fashion as follows:

Cap Rate = Annual Net Operating Income/Cost (or Value)

As an example, let's assume a building is bought for $1 million, and that during the following 12 months after the sale the property produces $100,000 in positive net operating income (this is the amount left over after fixed costs and variable costs are subtracted from gross lease income). In this case, the calculation would be as follows:

$$\$100,000 \; / \; \$1,000,000 = 0.10 = 10\%$$

In this case, the cap rate is 10 percent.

Now, we've told you that the triple net market is driven by the capitalization rate, and many investors focus exclusively on this rate as a measure of a property's value. But while the calculation is important, it's not the only measure, and it may not tell the whole story about an investment. Here's an example to illustrate this very important point:

"Mr. Thompson," a triple net investor client, is looking for a long term, passive, low risk investment. His mindset is that he doesn't want to think about the investment for as long as possible. He simply wants to get a wire transfer of money to his account each month.

During his search, he finds a Walgreens Drug store with a 25-year triple net lease and the option to renew the lease for up to an additional 50 years. This means Mr. Thompson may have income on the property for up to 75 years. It also means he's found exactly the right investment for the following reasons:

- It is stable because Walgreens has a very high credit rating.
- The lease term is long.
- The lease is absolute triple net, but there are no rental increases in the lease for the entire term of the lease, so there's potentially 75 years of the exact same rent.

This works for Mr. Thompson (and a lot of investors) because of the passivity of the investment and the ease of transfer of this type of asset to future generations. However, the triple net investor has to be comfortable with not getting a rental increase, ever.

How does this work? Well, let's assume the cost of the Walgreens store was $6 million, and Mr. Thompson will receive rent of $465,000 a year for the entire term of the lease.

The cap rate is 7.75%. Now, if Mr. Thompson were interested in something less stable, he could take some investment risk and buy a less desirable triple net property.

For example, let's say he decided to buy a local restaurant located on the best corner in town. It's a two-acre parcel with access from two streets. It's also at a lighted intersection, it's visible from many directions, and there is the ability to expand on the adjoining land.

The local restaurant has been at this location for about 40 years, but sales have been declining due to the owners' inactivity. They'd like to retire since they can't put as much effort into the restaurant. They feel that within the next two years they'd like to either sell the business to someone else or close it altogether.

So, the restaurant owners decide to do a two-year sale-leaseback where they agree to a two-year triple net lease with Mr. Thompson and, at the end of the two years, the tenants will vacate the property.

Mr. Thompson agrees to pay $3 million for the parcel with the restaurant and receive rent of $180,000 year from the restaurant owners for two years at a 6 percent cap rate. So, with the cap rate being lower and the risk higher since it's a short-term lease with a non-credit tenant, what could the upside be for Mr. Thompson?

Well, in this case, the restaurant owners retired two years later and then closed the restaurant. At that point, our triple net lease investor, Mr. Thompson, owned a two-acre parcel on the best corner in town. Essentially, he's already got replacement tenants lining up to put a store on his location.

This investor signed a 20-year ground lease with a tenant, with 20 years of renewal options with a very high credit-rated bank. And the tenants liked the location so much they were willing to pay $300,000 a year in rent with 10 percent rental increases every five years.

Essentially, the 6% cap rate became a 10% cap rate for Mr. Thompson, who would receive $300,000 year on his $3 million investment. Therefore, it may make sense to take a calculated risk with a lesser-known tenant if the quality of the real estate is very good, and the investor knows that he or she could make more money at a later date.

The point of the case study above was to illustrate the fact that the cap rate isn't everything. You can buy a great piece of real estate that has a terrible tenant and a short-term lease. You'd think that the cap rate would be high because the credit and lease are not good.

But the real estate is so good that you almost want the tenant to default so you can get a better tenant and a longer-term lease. McDonald's and other national tenants use this strategy quite a bit with their locations, where they select an old gas station site or an old restaurant site because the real estate is ideally suited for their business needs.

So, here's the key point: As an investor, you should weigh all the options and not focus solely on the capitalization rate.

Cash-on-Cash Return

There are two other important areas you should consider in addition to the capitalization rate: cash-on-cash return and loan assumptions.

This "cash-on-cash" phrase refers to a simple, but very important formula that allows you to evaluate the long-term performance of a triple net lease property investment (and other types of property investments, as well). Here's the formula:

$$\text{Annual Net Cash Flow} \div \text{Net Investment} = \text{Cash-on-Cash Return}$$

Here's an example that illustrates the use of the formula: Assume the net cash flow from a property is $20,000, and the cash invested in the property is $200,000. The cash on cash return would then be 10 percent, ($20,000/$200,000).

Keep in mind that this formula doesn't include property appreciation, which is considered a non-cash flow item until the year of sale. Since, in this case, you're evaluating a property on a long-term basis, you need to zero in on the annual cash flow as it relates to your investment rather than on property appreciation.

Loan Assumption

A loan assumption is exactly what it sounds like – you assume a mortgage loan from a seller/borrower and take on the resultant loan obligations. There are benefits to this approach. If credit is tight, for example, you can take on a loan without all the normal, time-consuming paperwork that comes with getting a new loan. Under the right circumstances, this means you can finish the whole transaction faster and cheaper and, thus, get the income stream flowing that much sooner.

However, the realization of these benefits often depends on the complexity of the transaction. Highly complicated deals will naturally take more time and effort. The length or complexity of the assumption process will also depend on the type of loan and lender involved. For instance, if the loan in question is structured as a commercial mortgage-backed security, the process will more complicated and time-consuming.

Also, the loan to be assumed must be examined with a fine-toothed comb to ensure that the provisions meet your needs. Often, these provisions are subject to negotiation.

Step by Step Process

Now let's look in detail at the steps mentioned at the beginning of the chapter so you can understand exactly what happens as part of the "due diligence" process in the evaluation of triple net lease investments.

Step 1: Evaluate the Real Estate

The purpose of this step is to do an initial evaluation of the property in terms of its potential for a triple net investment. If everything goes well, then a contract is signed, and an in-depth evaluation ("due diligence") is performed. (Due diligence will be covered in detail in the next chapter of this book.)

During Step 1, these tasks must be completed:

- On-site property visits
- Salient fact identification

- Surrounding residential and commercial development detection
- Analysis of physical characteristics, etc.

As you can see, there are many variables that come into play during this initial stage. Depending on the nature of the business and the location, for example, the questions you'll want to ask during the on-site property visits will vary. For example, environmental issues might not be a big factor with an established pharmacy site; however, they could be a potentially very expensive factor in terms of an industrial "dirty" industry involving chemical, petroleum products and such. It's not within the scope of this book to cover in exhaustive detail every aspect of the real estate evaluation process in Step 1, but below are a few of the potentially troublesome and expensive areas that must be analyzed carefully before a deal is ever made.

Easements give one party the right to go onto another party's property, often either to pass through it or make use of a portion of the property itself. Before investing in a property, be sure to check on the easement situation. If a tenant erects a retail store on a piece of property, for example, only to find that he or she can't expand a parking lot because it runs smack dab up against a neighbor business' easement rights, then the situation can get difficult, to say the least. A thorough investigation by the investment team and counsel is necessary in this situation. Sometimes, items are missed on surveys or contracts. The team should check with the city public works and building department to ensure that no nasty easement issues will crop up in the future.

Encroachments are protrusions from another property onto the property you're considering. For example, perhaps the original property line was not surveyed properly, and you find that, say, the next-door building has placed a big, ugly dumpster on it. That's a fairly easy problem to take care of. Encroachments get harder to resolve when underground installations such fuel tanks, septic tanks and other such systems are involved. Naturally, you wouldn't want potentially hazardous installations on your property, but it's entirely possible you'll have to go to court to get the matter resolved, and that can cost you a lot of money and time. That's why it's vital for the team to closely check surveys or to have another survey done.

Environmental Inspections are another important area to check closely for the simple reason that environmental clean-up can be a huge expense, depending on the nature of the problem. A partial list of typical issues includes:

- Lead paint
- Ground water contamination
- Asbestos insulation
- PCBs

If you buy a property that's plagued by these issues, and unless a clear indemnification is outlined in the lease, then you'll be liable for the cleanup in many instances, even though you had nothing to do with the original problem.

To add insult to injury, your property's resale potential will plummet. Frankly, such problems break the back of many deals. However, if the investment team does decide the deal is worth doing, it should stipulate that the current owner clean up the problem before the property is purchased.

Our best advice is this: firms that have considerable experience and expertise in this area should conduct an environmental analysis. These companies should have individuals who are certified in their particular environmental area.

Step 2: Evaluate the Creditworthiness of the Tenant

This is obviously a vital step that needs to be done early in the evaluation process. Signing a lease with a tenant whose credit is suspect or shaky is simply asking for financial trouble and personal headaches.

An initial credit investigation by the investment team and other rating agencies should include facts and figures from the following sources:

- Securities and Exchange Commission information (public companies do their reporting through the SEC)
- Standard and Poor's, Moody's, Fitch, NAIC, etc.

- Financial statements
- Tax returns
- Sales figures
- Full credit report (including a minimum of three years of historical data)
- Credit references, etc.

Before getting into the specifics of creditworthiness, we'd like to provide you with a few real-life examples of triple net lease investments and how their credit is rated and affected by the structure of particular businesses:

Example 1: Taco Bell

In terms of creditworthiness, there are essentially two types of guarantees with this company. First, there are the corporate Taco Bells owned by Yum! Brands. These are easy to underwrite because of the corporation's high credit rating and the ready availability of information on the company.

The second guarantee involves Taco Bell franchisees. These are privately owned companies (e.g. Taco Bell Alabama LLC). In this case, the franchisee guarantees the lease, not Yum! Brands. As such, they don't necessarily have the credit rating of a corporate Taco Bell or information on them that's easily available.

Typically, of course, investors want the Yum! Brand, corporate-guaranteed Taco Bell investment. But, if they need to go with a franchisee, they'll require a higher return because of the higher risk due to the lower credit of the franchisee.

Example 2: Blue Cross Blue Shield of Florida

This firm has an S&P investment grade rating of A+, which is an extremely strong credit rating. Now, Blue Cross isn't well known in the net lease industry because they don't have a ton of retail centers. However, they own a lot of real estate. This, plus their high credit rating, makes them potentially an attractive investment.

Example 3: Walgreens

34

Walgreens has a Standard and Poor's rating of A+. Because of this excellent credit rating, investors are willing to sign a very lengthy lease (20-75 years) that doesn't change the rent at all, including the renewal option periods. Needless to say, this is a very popular tenant.

Example 4: Pep Boys

Pep Boys has a single B credit rating. Statistically, there's a 40% chance of them defaulting over a 5-year period. In such cases, the investor wants to be rewarded for the higher risk. Therefore, the cap rates are commensurately higher than, say, a Walgreens store.

These examples should give you an idea of various triple net lease investments and how they earn their overall creditworthiness. Of course, when dealing with individual tenants, you'll always want to dig deeper. As the old saying goes, the devil is in the details.

If, for instance, a potential tenant has a firm that was founded less than 12 months ago, then you'll want to investigate any former companies that the firm's principals were involved with. Also, it never hurts to review a new firm's business plan and investigate the overall strength of the industry in which the company operates.

If the investment team is dealing with smaller, privately held firms or partnerships, then it's essential to get personal credit reports on all principals as well. Background and experience are helpful indicators too, since the company may be solid in terms of its credit, but one or more of the principals could have personal problems. One owner, for example, might have past bankruptcies, late payments, considerable credit card debt, or other issues. If that's the case and you still want to pursue the deal, then you may want to seek personal guarantees from the principals.

The investment team shouldn't take tenants who are subsidiaries of a larger company at face value. The tenant may be solid, but what about the financial resources of the parent corporation as well? Are they substantial? Or, in another case, the subsidiary tenant may have questionable credit. If so, then the team may want to seek a corporate guarantee for all or part of the lease term from the parent company.

It's ideal when both vendor and customer references hold a positive view of the tenant company. The tenant will (or should) gladly provide them to you, but it's up to the investment team to check out references independently as well.

Here's a red flag to watch out for: As part of reviewing credit reports and information, the investment team should note how a company pays its bills. For example, does it pay within 60 days or are the payments stretching out to 90 or 100 days or more? This can be an indication of financial problems. If that's the case, the investment team should consider making a request for a letter of credit, a corporate guarantee, or increased security deposit before any papers are signed.

Also consider the tenant's recent sales history. If sales have declined, the team needs to determine what the cause of the problem is. For example, is the decline due to a regional recession and a troubled industry as a whole, or is it confined to the individual company? If the sales decline is small during a recession, then the investment team shouldn't weight that variable very heavily (knowing that many companies are likely to be suffering the effects of the economic downturn). On the other hand, if the market is faring well, and if the tenant company is still losing market share, then that's definitely a red flag for future financial trouble. (Credit bureaus are of great help in this situation since they can compare a prospective tenant's performance to comparable businesses in the same field.)

In the best of all possible worlds, the investment team will be able to audit and evaluate the tenant company's business plan, financial statements, tax returns, and sales reports for the last two or three years. This can provide evidence of a solid financial footing. It's important to note that audits are always preferable but this may be too expensive for smaller companies. Just because reports have not been audited doesn't mean that financial problems exist.

Now, if a tenant is a public company, then the team should review annual reports, required regulatory filings, and the rating issued for the company by the appropriate rating agencies. The team can also gather valuable information on a company's structure and stability via corporate charters and Uniform Commercial Code filings (available from each state's Secretary of State).

Public records are another source for potential red flags in regard to creditworthiness. For example, there may be bankruptcies, suits, and judgments against the company (or its principals).

Finally, from an investor's point of view, it's wise to monitor the tenant's financial health on a yearly basis. For example, a tenant may want to renew or expand, both of which can change its finances, and not always for the better. If possible, the investor should request annual financial reports and tax returns. Of course, it's always wise to keep tabs on the tenant's industry as to what the trends are.

Keep alert for red flags indicating financial troubles (e.g., slow rent payment, improbable excuses for non-payment, and lack of communication), on an ongoing basis. These indicators may push the investor to conduct a thorough review of a tenant's finances, which in a worst-case scenario situation can result in eviction or non-renewal of the lease.

To illustrate how important it is to monitor a tenant's financial health, here's an example in which an investor didn't pursue this ongoing "due diligence" and paid the price:

A triple net lease investor bought an industrial "flex" property in the eastern United States after completing the necessary due diligence. The property comprised 24,000 square feet, 5,000 of it office and the rest warehouse space. A Fortune 100 company that supplied fireplaces and other products to homebuilders occupied the property. The tenant had an extremely high credit rating.

It looked like a great investment, so the investor bought the building with four years left on the lease. He also paid a price for the facility below its replacement value; that is, it cost more to build the building at that time than what he actually bought it for. Remember that back in 2006 the home-building industry was doing extremely well, so the landlord didn't think too much about maintaining communication with the tenant company.

As the market worsened in 2007-08, the tenant's sales dropped dramatically. All of a sudden, the company started to complain about the state of the building (e.g., leaky roof, etc.), and the investor-landlord had to remind them that the triple net lease stipulated that, as tenant, they were responsible for the maintenance of the building.

In reality, the tenant was trying to get out of the building in order to consolidate locations because of dismal sales. They stopped paying rent and moved out of the building. This resulted in a suit and countersuit for approximately $500,000 each. Through arbitration and after paying legal costs, etc., the client got about three month's rent ($40,000).

However, because the client wasn't monitored regularly, the investor-landlord paid a heavy price for his neglect. He wound up with an empty building on which he had to continue paying the mortgage (without any income). As a result, he had to take about $70,000 out of pocket to pay the mortgage, even more money to hire a leasing broker to find a new tenant, and more yet to pay for maintenance required by the new tenant because the previous tenant had failed to keep the place up.

Here's the moral of this story: Always pay attention to a tenant's market and financial condition and to his or her maintenance of the building. Don't just sit back and collect the rent; otherwise, you may get a nasty surprise.

Keep the tenant accountable throughout the term of the lease, short or long term!

Step 3: Evaluate the Lease

The elements of a triple net lease agreement will vary, of course, with the particular property and the particular deal. However, there is one constant to a triple net lease agreement (or any other lease, for that matter) – it should be written in clear language so that there's no ambiguity to its terms. There's a basic business and legal reason for this: when the language is unclear or confusing, it lays the groundwork for potential future disagreements between the parties.

An attorney is critical at this juncture. These are very detailed documents, and a layperson should seek counsel.

That's why leases of any kind must be gone over with the proverbial fine-toothed comb. Potential areas of disagreement need to be identified and discussed before any papers are signed. Your investment team should also make sure that the lease meets your investment objectives.

There's no doubt that the lease can make or break any deal! It must be read and/or written with care. Otherwise, you may become the owner of a lease with provisions that can be hard to live with and extremely costly. These provisions could involve anything from the roof and the building structure to the parking lot, taxes, insurance, HVAC, and so forth.

As you can see, your investment team should take the utmost care in the evaluation of triple net leases. And, if you're in a position where you need to evaluate a lease on your own, then take the very same steps your team would take:

1) Read every word of the lease and make notes on items you don't understand or need to clarify.
2) Have someone else repeat the same process; for example, an attorney or other expert in the area of triple net leases.
3) Compare notes.
4) Seek answers to your questions and make a decision based on the clarity of the answers (and all other investment factors, of course).

These are just general rules. Here's a more specific rule of thumb in terms of the value of a triple net lease: The more passive the lease to the landlord, the higher the value of the property; the more the landlord has to do, the lower the property value. If there's an absolutely passive lease in which the tenant takes care of everything (taxes, insurance, maintenance, etc.), it's typically valued at a higher level because all the landlord has to do is to receive a rent check.

On the other hand, if the landlord has to maintain or repair the roof, building, etc., then the landlord must set aside a reserve of money to pay for those expenses. The landlord will want to be compensated for that money, so the cap rate and return increase (due to the added expenses for the landlord). Here's an example to illustrate this situation:

Assume there's a double net lease in which the tenant is responsible for the roof, the building structure, and so forth. In the course of events, the parking lot has to be re-striped and a leaky roof has to be fixed at the landlord's expense. This takes away from the landlord's net operating income (rent).

Also, the investment team has to make sure there's no opportunity for the tenant to get out of a lease. In some cases, the tenant has the right to cancel the lease if they're not performing well (occasionally linked to sales).

When that happens, the landlord is left waiting for the building to become vacant. So, in effect, termination options devalue the property. Therefore, the investment team should know what the termination options are and what they're based on.

Step 4: Compare and Analyze the Information from Steps 1-3

Once your team has completed Steps 1 through 3, it should gather all of the information and analyze it to determine deal potential. By combining this information with all other considerations and recommendations, the team should be able to determine the net operating income or NOI, the most critical element in figuring out your return potential on the real estate investment.

Since NOI is so important, let's take a closer look at exactly what it means and the value it represents for investors.

The formula for calculating NOI is straightforward. Net operating income is equal to a property's yearly gross income minus operating expenses or:

$$\text{Gross Income} - \text{Operating Expenses} = \text{NOI}$$

Gross income comprises all income associated with a property. Depending on the nature of the property, this can include rental income and other income such as parking fees, laundry and vending receipts, etc.

Operating expenses are costs incurred during the operation and maintenance of a property. Again, depending on the nature of a property, these expenses can include repairs and maintenance, insurance, management fees, utilities, supplies, property taxes, and so forth.

Operating expenses typically don't include such items as principal and interest, capital expenditures, depreciation, income taxes, and amortization of loan points. (The landlord should take out reserves for future operating expenses [5%, 10%, or cost per square foot]).

Here's how to calculate NOI on your potential investments:

Income

Gross Rents Possible:	$100,000
Less Vacancy and Reserves:	$2,000
Effective Gross Income	$98,000
Less Operating Expenses:	$31,000
Net Operating Income:	$67,000

Let's say your investment team is evaluating a similar income property that's currently for sale with a net operating income of $500,000. You'd estimate the value of this property with a 10 percent cap rate like this:

Net Operating Income: $500,000

Estimated Value = $500,000 / 0.10 = $5,000,000

Summary

From this chapter you can see how vital it is for your investment team to dig deeply into each potential deal and put every aspect of the properties and the triple net leases under a microscope. This allows the team to spot the best opportunities and avoid the ones with potential financial pitfalls.

Once a great opportunity is selected, then it's time to take the next step: write and send a letter of intent. We'll walk you through that process in the next chapter.

The Letter of Intent

As the name suggests, a letter of intent (LOI) is a non-binding means of expressing your intention to buy a property (or a lease). Think of it as a basis for starting a conversation with a seller. That is, you're letting him or her know in simple, clear language that you'd like to buy a property, how you'd like to purchase it, and under what terms. An LOI is comes before the negotiation and signing of a contract (assuming all parties agree).

The following points are typically covered in an LOI:

Purchase Price

The initial purchase price is stated, so both sides have a starting point for negotiations on this subject.

Conditions

This section stipulates the conditions that must be met during the due diligence period (before the final contract is signed). The conditions will vary with the deal, of course. In our example at the end of this chapter, the conditions include an environmental inspection, review and audit of financial arrangements, title review, etc.

Take note that the due diligence period will vary with the complexity of the project. A straightforward deal with, say, one building and a single income stream, for instance, can be closed easily within the 30-day period. A complex one, on the other hand, can take much longer due to the nuances that need to be considered (e.g., multiple buildings and multiple income streams).

Closing

A specific closing date or time period is stated in this section "after waiver of all contingencies." In other words, all contingencies have been satisfactorily met.

Closing Costs

Closing costs are outlined in this section as well who is responsible for paying them. Often, the buyer will be responsible for X amount of costs, while the seller is responsible for another portion of them. These costs can be substantial.

Prorations

This is simply a method of dividing the financial responsibility for various areas between a buyer and seller in many real estate transactions. These include such areas as:

- Real estate taxes/assessments
- Rents
- Security deposits
- Security contracts, etc.

Brokers

This section specifies who the brokers are, and which broker is representing the buyer and which one is representing the seller. It also specifies the amount of the commission to be paid at closing.

Deposit

Generally speaking, the buyer will put a specific amount of money into escrow upon signing of the purchase agreement. In our example (later in this chapter), that figure is $25,000. Then, as you can see, this section specifies that the buyer will deposit an additional $75,000 upon satisfaction of all contingencies at the end of the due diligence period. Such terms are fairly standard for triple net lease deals.

Assignment

This section states that the buyer has the right to transfer and assign the purchase agreement to another person or institution (to be formed) of his or her choice: e.g., a partnership, corporation, Limited Liability Company, etc.

Tax Free Exchange

Since we've indicated elsewhere in this book that triple net leases are often used as part of the government's 1031 exchange option, this contingency is often included in a letter of intent. Basically, it states that the seller will help the buyer complete the exchange within the required time period.

Other Considerations

Finally, in the example that follows, we specify that the LOI is, "not intended to create a legal commitment binding upon either seller or purchaser." This makes it clear to the intended party that the letter of intent is simply a means for further discussion and nothing else. In other words, it's a legally executable, but non-binding document.

Assuming that upon receipt of the Letter of Intent, the seller wants to proceed, then it's time to move to the Purchase Agreement stage, which is the subject of the next chapter.

Sample Letter of Intent

May 3, 2010

Re: Letter of Intent to Purchase

Dear _____:

I am pleased to present from _____ the following Letter of Intent proposal to purchase the property known as _____ located in _____.

If the General Provisions set forth below are acceptable, then it is the intention of both parties to negotiate the remaining terms to enter into a real estate purchase contract (the "Purchase Contract") within fourteen (14) days from the date of Purchaser's and Seller's execution of this Letter of Intent.

1. Purchase Price: $_____

2. Conditions: For a period of thirty (30) days following the execution of the Purchase Contract ("Due Diligence") Purchaser's obligation to close shall be contingent upon the following.

a.   Satisfactory results of a Phase I Environmental inspection. If there is a recent existing environmental inspection, Seller shall provide a copy to Purchaser for his review.

b.   Purchaser's satisfactory review and audit of financial arrangements, tenants financial statement and any and all other contractual obligations and other matters affecting the property and its operation, that are available to the Seller including operator's expenses and establishing an accurate and acceptable net operating income.

c.   Satisfactory title review and applicable easements.

d.   Satisfactory survey results.

e.   Satisfactory physical inspection of the property, building plans and its surrounding location.

f.   Purchaser's satisfaction that the proper zoning is in effect and there are no zoning violations.

g.   Prior to expiration of the due diligence period, Purchaser shall deliver to Seller a letter either clearing all contingencies and establishing a date for closing or terminating the agreement. If Purchaser elects to terminate based on any of the conditions listed above, all earnest money deposits shall be returned to Purchaser.

3. Closing: Closing shall take place within thirty (30) days after waiver of all contingencies referred to above, but no later than _____, 2010.

46

4. Closing Costs: All closing costs shall be charged accordingly to practices normal to the State of_____.

5. Prorations: The customary prorations are to be made as of the closing date including, without limitation, the following, if applicable: real estate taxes and assessments, rents, security deposits, security contracts. Any prorations to which Purchaser may be entitled by reason of the foregoing shall be credited against the balance of the purchase price to be paid at closing.

6a. Brokers: Each party shall warrant to the other that no real estate brokers or other intermediary was involved in connection with bringing about this transaction contemplated hereby other than (broker name). A commission in the amount of _____ percent (____%) will be paid by seller at closing.

6b. Deposit: Purchaser shall deposit Twenty-Five Thousand and 00/100 Dollars ($25,000) in escrow upon signing a Purchase & Sale contract. Upon satisfaction of all contingencies at the end of the Due Diligence period, Purchaser shall deposit an additional Fifty Thousand and 00/100 Dollars ($50,000) for a total of Seventy-Five Thousand and 00/100 Dollars ($75,000) in escrow, which will become non-refundable after satisfactory completion of Due Diligence.

1   Assignment: Purchaser shall have the right to transfer and assign the purchase agreement to another or others of his choice including, but not limited to, a Limited Liability Company, partnership or corporation to be formed.

2   Tax Free Exchange: Purchaser intends to purchase this property in connection with a tax-free exchange as contemplated in Section 1031 of the IRS Code. Seller agrees to cooperate with Purchaser to affect the exchange, including accommodation of scheduling closing to ensure closing for this property occurs after Purchaser's initial sale closing. Purchaser will pay all expenses associated with the tax-free exchange.

This letter is not intended to create a legal commitment binding upon either Seller or Purchaser. It is understood that this letter is intended to outline the principal terms of a proposed agreement for the purchase and sale of the subject property, upon which the Purchaser will instruct his attorney to proceed with drafting a Purchase Contract.

If the foregoing is acceptable to Seller, please so indicate by signing this letter in the space provided below and returning to me no later than _____, 2010.

Sincerely, (Name of broker)

ACCEPTANCE:

Purchaser:
By: _____ Date: _____

Seller:
By: _____ Date: _____

The Purchase Agreement

In commercial real estate deals, a contract is also commonly referred to as a "purchase agreement." These agreements are a different animal from the residential contracts you may be familiar with. Quite often, the latter are relatively simple form documents drawn up by a real estate agent and signed by all parties.

In the case of triple net leases (and other commercial real estate deals), a purchase agreement is a negotiated item, with attorneys for each side involved to a greater or lesser degree, depending on the complexity of the issues. Of course, such agreements are legally binding documents.

Be aware that brokers such as Calkain and others are not attorneys. As such, they aren't involved in any of the legal matters involving contracts. The legality of purchase agreements is not negotiated by either the purchaser or the seller, but by the respective attorneys. Those attorneys, in turn, use the proper contract structure and nomenclature for whatever state they're operating in. Often, it will be determined upfront as to which party will draft the initial contract. The selected attorneys will use a contract form they're comfortable with.

Typically, attorneys advise only on the legal issues and reconcile differing legal opinions on the transaction. Otherwise, business matters like pricing and timing are left up to the buyer and seller.

When the initial contract is drawn up, the Letter of Intent serves as the outline. The purchase agreement basically expands on each of the different points in the LOI, and spells them out in a formal manner (as you can see in the example at the end of this chapter).

While the contract forms vary with the transaction, there are some typical elements, including the recitals section, which gives an overview of the situation. For example, it:

- Describes the property in specific terms
- States that the buyer and seller wish to enter into a transaction for purchase and sale of the property
- Specifies that the seller is not selling the tenant improvements to the buyer

The agreement section comes next, and gets into the "nitty gritty" of the contract. First, the purchase price of $1.2 million is specified and how it will be paid:

- $25,000 earnest money paid within three business days after the commencement date
- $75,000 additional deposit within two business days of the termination of the feasibility period
- Balance paid at closing

Then the feasibility study particulars are outlined. This section specifies a period (30 days) within which the study will take place. It also states the purchaser has the right to enter the property to conduct:

- Feasibility studies
- Financial analyses
- Environmental studies
- Financing inquiries
- Appraisals
- Title searches
- Any and all tests

Next, the purchase agreement stipulates in paragraph B that the buyer agrees to indemnify the seller against any claims, damages, etc., arising from the buyer's entry into the property.

In paragraph C, it's stipulated that the buyer can terminate the agreement if he or she is unsatisfied for any reason with the results of the feasibility study, or if the purchaser is unable to procure funding. It also stipulates that the deposit be returned in full. The remainder of the paragraph spells out the conditions under which "objectionable defects" of a property can be "cured" by the seller, thus allowing the deal to either go forward or be terminated.

Next, the contract spells out the closing procedures and specifications, including:

- Closing date and site
- Conveyance of all necessary documents (special warranty deed, etc.)
- Payment of the purchase price
- Condemnation (conditions for handling in the event it occurs)
- Taxes and assessment (prorating)
- Default conditions (by either buyer or seller)
- Brokerage fees
- Assignments
- Closing costs

As you can see, every aspect of the transaction is spelled out as fully and clearly as possible in the contract. This protects the interests of both parties and can prevent future legal disputes. Once the purchase agreement is hashed out and agreed upon, it will be time for due diligence – the subject of the next chapter.

Sample Purchase Agreement

PURCHASE AGREEMENT

This PURCHASE AGREEMENT (the "Agreement"), dated April __, 2010, by and between XYZ, L.L.C., a (state) limited liability company (the "Seller") and ABC PROPERTY INVESTMENT PARTNERS, INC., a (state) corporation, and/or its assigns (the "Purchaser"), recites and provides as follows:

RECITALS:

A. The Seller owns that certain parcel of land known as 000 Limestone Ave. (Parcel Number 736-750-3663), totaling approximately 1.0 acre, (the "Property") as more particularly shown or described on the plat entitled "Compiled Plat Showing Two Parcels of Land Lying on the South Line of Limestone Ave.," by _____ P.C., dated August 24, 2004, and attached hereto as Exhibit "A" and by this reference made a part hereof. The purchase and sale of the Property is subject to the existing Deed of Ground Lease dated November 23, 2004, as amended (the "Lease") between Seller, as lessor, and DEF Bank, as lessee (the "Tenant").

B. Purchaser desires to purchase and Seller agrees to sell the Property subject to the terms and provisions of this Agreement.

C. Pursuant to the Lease with Tenant, the building improvements and other improvements constructed by Tenant on the land (collectively, "Tenant Improvements ") are the property of the Tenant, and the term "Property" as used herein does not include the Tenant Improvements. Seller is not selling the Tenant Improvements to Purchaser.

AGREEMENT:

NOW, THEREFORE, for and in consideration of the mutual promises, covenants and conditions set forth herein, and other good and valuable consideration, the receipt and sufficiency of which are hereby mutually acknowledged, the parties hereto agree as follows:

1.   Sale and Purchase. Subject to the terms and conditions hereof, Seller shall sell and Purchaser shall purchase the Property. The last date upon which the parties execute this Agreement hereto shall be hereinafter referred to as the "Commencement Date".

2.   Purchase Price. The purchase price for the Property shall be ONE MILLION TWO HUNDRED TWENTY FIVE THOUSAND AND NO/100 DOLLARS ($1,225,000.00) (the "Purchase Price"). The Purchase Price shall be payable as follows:

A. Twenty Five Thousand and No/100 Dollars ($25,000.00) earnest money deposit shall be paid by the Purchaser to Purchaser's attorney, Joe J., 3081 Blaise Ave, Building D, Suite 104, (city, state, ZIP code), within three (3) business days after the Commencement Date and deposited in an interest bearing account (the "Initial Deposit") with interest accruing and following the Initial Deposit;

B. If the Purchaser does not terminate the Agreement during the Feasibility Period as provided below, a Seventy Five Thousand and No/100 Dollars ($75,000.00) additional deposit (the "Additional Deposit") shall be paid by the Purchaser to Purchaser's attorney within two (2) business days of the termination of the Feasibility Period, and the Additional Deposit shall be deposited in an interest bearing account (the Initial Deposit and Additional Deposit are collectively referred to herein as the "Deposit") with interest accruing and following the Deposit, and the Deposit shall be nonrefundable to Purchaser except in the event of a default by Seller or as expressly set forth herein;

C. The balance of the Purchase Price shall be paid by wire transfer at Closing, as hereinafter defined; and

D. The Deposit shall be applicable to the Purchase Price.

3. Feasibility Study.

A. For a period of thirty (30) days from the latter of (a) the Commencement Date; or

(b) the date that Purchaser receives the Seller Deliverables, as hereinafter defined (the "Feasibility Period"), Purchaser shall have the right to enter onto the Property at reasonable times and subject to the rights of Tenant under the Lease, to conduct any and all feasibility studies and financial analyses, environmental studies, financing inquiries, appraisals, title searches, surveys, and any and all other tests, studies and analyses (the "Studies"), which Purchaser determines are necessary in order to determine the feasibility of this transaction.

B. Purchaser agrees to indemnify against and hold Seller harmless from any claims, demands, damages, losses, liabilities, suits, actions, costs and expenses, including, without limitation, reasonable attorney's fees, arising out of or in connection with or related to any entry upon the Property by Purchaser, or any agents, contractors, or employees of Purchaser. Purchaser, at its own expense, shall promptly repair any damage to the Property caused by any of its Studies. Purchaser's indemnity and repair obligations under this paragraph shall survive termination of or Closing under this Agreement.

C. In the event that Purchaser determines that Purchaser is unsatisfied for any reason with the results of any Studies or Purchaser is unable to procure financing, Purchaser may, upon written notice to the Seller within the Feasibility Period, (a) terminate this Agreement by written notice to Seller given within the Feasibility Period, in which event this Agreement shall then be deemed terminated, the Deposit shall be returned in full to the Purchaser, and neither Seller nor Purchaser shall have any further obligation to one another hereunder except those that expressly survive termination hereunder, or (b) notify the Seller of any objectionable defects (the "Objections," which term shall include title and survey objections); and, thereafter, the Seller shall have a period of ten (10) days to notify the Purchaser in writing whether or not it elects to cure the Objections. If the Seller elects to cure the Objections, the Seller shall have a reasonable time to cure the Objections, but in no event later than the date of Closing or as may otherwise be agreed upon by the parties hereto. If the Seller elects not to cure the Objections or fails to notify Purchaser within the required ten (10) day period of its option to cure, the Purchaser shall have the right to either

(a) terminate this Agreement by written notice to Seller given within five (5) days after Seller's election not to cure or the expiration of such ten (10) day period, as applicable, in which event this Agreement shall then be deemed terminated, the Deposit shall be returned in full to the Purchaser, and neither Seller nor Purchaser shall have any further obligation to one another hereunder except those that expressly survive termination, or (b) waive the Objections and proceed to Closing as set forth in this Agreement, with no reduction in the Purchase Price.

D. Seller shall deliver to Purchaser no later than five (5) business days after the Commencement Date, copies of the Lease with any and all amendments, the liability insurance policy required per the Lease, all engineering and environmental studies in Seller's possession, all surveys in Seller's possession, any easement or cross-access agreements related to the Property in Seller's possession, and Seller's most recent title insurance policy (the "Seller Deliverables"). Purchaser acknowledges that studies, reports, and surveys related to the Property are furnished as an accommodation to Purchaser, and Seller makes no representation or warranty as to the completeness or accuracy thereof.

4. Closing.

A. Closing of the purchase and sale of the Property shall take place at Purchaser's attorney's office on the date that is thirty (30) days after the end of the Feasibility Period, TIME BEING OF THE ESSENCE (the "Closing").

B. At the Closing, Seller shall convey to Purchaser, by special warranty deed in a form reasonably acceptable to Purchaser (the "Deed"), fee simple title to the Property free and clear of any and all liens, encumbrances, conditions or restrictions required under Section 3C to be cured by Seller. Seller shall deliver possession of the Property to the Purchaser as of the date of Closing subject only to the Lease, which shall be assigned by Seller to Purchaser at Closing pursuant to an assignment of lease (the "Assignment"). The Assignment shall provide that (i) the Seller assigns the Lease to Purchaser as of the date of Closing; (ii) the Purchaser assumes the obligations of Seller as lessor under the Lease arising on and after the date of Closing; (iii) Seller and Purchaser each indemnifies, defends, and holds harmless the other from and against all claims, causes of action, losses, damages, liabilities, costs and expenses, including, without limitation, reasonable attorneys fees, arising during its period of ownership; and (iv) Purchaser specifically assumes Seller's obligation to pay (name), monthly, a commission of five percent (5%) of the gross rent, as such rent is collected, from the Tenant under the Lease, Seller hereby disclosing such commission to Purchaser and Purchaser hereby agreeing to assume such commission obligation as of and after Closing.

C. At the Closing, Seller also shall deliver to Purchaser all documents reasonably requested by Purchaser, including, without limitation, a 1099-S filing form, a FIRPTA affidavit, a (state) Resident Reporting Form, an Owner's Affidavit as to Mechanic's Liens and Possession subject to the Lease and reasonably acceptable to Purchaser and Purchaser's title company, and the Assignment. Seller shall deliver a subordination and non-disturbance agreement in the form provided in the Lease a Tenant estoppel certificate as provided in the Lease to Purchaser at closing containing an acknowledgement by Tenant that its right of first refusal under the Lease has expired and is of no further force and effect. If Seller is unable to deliver at Closing either a subordination and non-disturbance agreement or Tenant estoppel certificate from Tenant which contains such acknowledgement concerning the right of first refusal, then either party may terminate this Agreement by delivering written notice to the other party of same, whereupon neither Seller nor Purchaser shall have any further obligation to one another hereunder except those that expressly survive termination of this Agreement and the Purchaser's attorney shall return the Deposit in full to the Purchaser.

D. At the Closing, Purchaser shall pay the cash portion of the Purchase Price and execute and deliver the Assignment.

5. Condemnation. If, prior to or on the Closing, all or any part of the Property shall be condemned by governmental or other lawful authority, Purchaser shall have the option of: (a) completing the purchase, in which event all condemnation proceeds or claims thereof shall be assigned to Purchaser, or (b) terminating this Agreement, in which event this Agreement shall be terminated, neither Seller nor Purchaser shall then have any further obligation to one another hereunder except those that expressly survive termination of this Agreement, and the Purchaser's attorney shall return the Deposit in full to the Purchaser.

6. Taxes and Assessments. Real property taxes, water rates, sewer charges, and rent shall be prorated and adjusted to the date of Closing. Seller holds no Tenant security deposits under the Lease. Taxes for all prior years shall be paid by Seller, including "rollback" taxes. Assessments, either general or special, for improvements completed prior to the date of Closing and any common area maintenance (CAM) fees shall be prorated as of the date of Closing.

7. Default by Purchaser. If Purchaser shall default in the performance of any terms and conditions of this Agreement, or if the Closing shall not occur because of the fault of Purchaser, Seller may, as its sole and exclusive remedy, rescind this Agreement and the Purchaser's attorney shall deliver the Deposit to Seller as liquidated damages and Seller shall not have any other or additional right or remedy against the Purchaser. Notwithstanding the foregoing, in the event of a default by Purchaser under Section 3B or 9 hereof, Seller shall have all rights and remedies available at law or in equity.

8. Default by Seller. If Seller fails or refuses to comply fully with the terms of this Agreement, or any part hereof, and such failure or refusal continues for a period of five (5) business days after written notice thereof from Purchaser to Seller (no such notice and cure period to be applicable to Seller's obligation to convey the Property to Purchaser on the Closing Date), then Purchaser may elect, as its sole remedies to either (i) terminate this Agreement, in which event the Deposit shall be returned to the Purchaser on demand or (ii) enforce the provisions of this Agreement by specific performance.

9. Brokerage Fees. If Closing occurs, Seller shall pay at Closing a real estate commission fee of five percent (5%) of the Purchase Price to (name of real estate company), and Calkain Realty Advisors, LLC, to be divided equally between said agents. Other than (name of real estate company) and Calkain Realty Advisors, LLC, each party represents and warrants to the other that neither has taken any action which would give rise to a commission or brokerage fee being due as a result of the transfer of the Property and each party agrees to indemnify and hold the other party harmless from and against claims made for a commission due arising from such party's actions. The parties acknowledge that Calkain Realty Advisors, LLC has acted solely for Seller and (name of real estate company) has acted solely for Purchaser in this transaction.

10. Assignment. This Agreement, or any part thereof, may be assigned to any entity controlled by the persons who control Seller as of the date hereof. Purchaser may not assign this Agreement to any other party without the prior written consent of Seller. In no event shall any assignment relieve Purchaser of any liability hereunder.

11. Closing Costs. Notwithstanding anything to the contrary contained herein, the costs of Closing shall be paid as follows:

A. By Seller:

(1) Expenses of placing title in the condition required hereunder;

(2) Preparation of the Deed and other Seller's documents required hereunder including a Tenant subordination and non-disturbance agreement and Tenant estoppel certificate;

(3) Grantor's tax; and

(4) Seller's attorney's fees.

B. By Purchaser:

(1) Preparation of Purchaser documents required hereunder;

(2) Recording fees and Grantee's Tax;

(3) Title insurance examination and premium;

(4) Survey and any other investigations; and

(5) Purchaser's attorney's fees.

12. Risk of Loss. All risk of loss or damage to the Property by fire, windstorm, casualty or other cause is assumed by Seller until Closing.

13. Notices. All notices and demands which, under the terms of this Agreement, must or may be given by the parties hereto shall be delivered in person or sent by Federal Express or other comparable overnight courier, or certified mail, postage prepaid, return receipt requested, to the respective parties hereto as follows:

Notices shall be deemed to have been given when (a) delivered in person, (b) if sent by Federal Express or other comparable overnight courier, one (1) business day after deposit with such courier, courier fee prepaid, with receipt showing the correct name and address of the person to whom notice is to be given, and (c) if by certified mail, upon receipt if delivery is accepted, or if delivery is rejected, within three (3) days after depositing such notice in a United States Post Office or branch thereof.

1   Entire Agreement. This Agreement contains the entire agreement between Seller and Purchaser, and there are no other terms, conditions, promises, undertakings, statements or representations, expressed or implied, concerning the purchase and sale contemplated by this Agreement.

2   Modification. The terms of this Agreement may not be amended, waived or terminated orally, but only by an instrument in writing signed by Seller and Purchaser.

3   Successors. This Agreement shall inure to the benefit of and bind the parties hereto and their respective successors and assigns.

4   Counterparts; Facsimile. This Agreement may be executed in two or more counterparts, each of which shall be deemed an original, but all of which together shall constitute one of the same instrument. Seller and Purchaser agree that this Agreement may be transmitted between them by facsimile machine. Seller and Purchaser intend that faxed signatures shall constitute original signatures and that a faxed version of this Agreement containing the signatures (original or faxed) of Seller and Purchaser shall be binding on Seller and Purchaser.

5   1031 Exchange. Purchaser or Seller may elect to exchange for other real estate of a like kind in accordance with Section 1031 of the Internal Revenue Code of 1986 as amended. To the extent possible, the provisions of this paragraph shall be interpreted consistently with this intent. To exercise any rights under this paragraph, the party electing to exchange shall provide the other with a written statement stating its intent to enter into an exchange at least three (3) days prior to Closing. Either party's election to exchange, rather than sell or buy, for other real estate of a like kind shall be at no cost or liability to the other.

6   Captions. The captions and section headings contained herein are for convenience only and shall not be used in construing or enforcing any of the provisions of this Agreement.

7   Prevailing Party. If either party commences an action or arbitration against the other party arising out of or in connection with this Agreement, the substantially prevailing party shall be entitled to have and recover from the other party reasonable attorney's fees and costs of the action and/or arbitration.

8   Acceptance. This Agreement when executed on behalf of Purchaser shall be deemed an offer and shall remain in effect, unless withdrawn, until THREE (3) days following the date of offer shown below its signature or if none, the date Seller receives an executed copy of this Agreement. If not accepted by Seller within that time by delivery of a signed copy of this Agreement to the Purchaser, Purchaser shall have the right to withdraw such offer by notice to Seller, in which event this Agreement and the Purchaser's offer shall become null and void.

9   Governing Law. This Agreement and all documents and instruments referred to herein shall be governed by, and shall be construed according to, the laws of the Commonwealth of Virginia.

10   Incorporation by Reference. The exhibits identified herein and recitals are hereby incorporated by reference.

11   Arbitration. If a dispute arises between the parties relating to the interpretation or performance of this Agreement or the grounds for the termination thereof, the parties agree to meet to try to resolve the dispute. Such meeting shall be attended by individuals with decision-making authority to attempt, in good faith, to negotiate a resolution of the dispute prior to pursuing other available remedies. If, within thirty (30) days after such meeting, the parties have not resolved the dispute to their mutual satisfaction, the dispute shall be settled by arbitration in accordance with the Commercial Arbitration Rules of the American Arbitration Association currently in effect and such arbitration shall be final and binding. Arbitration shall be commenced ("Commencement") by written demand made in a timely manner by either party to the American Arbitration Association with a copy to the other party. Any written demand for arbitration will be deemed timely only if it is made before the date when institution of legal proceedings based upon such claim would be barred by the applicable statute of limitations in effect in the Commonwealth of Virginia. The arbitration shall be held in Richmond, Virginia and shall be heard by one (1) arbitrator. The arbitrator shall be selected by mutual agreement of the parties, or failing such agreement, by the American Arbitration Association. The award rendered by the arbitrator shall be based on a written and reasoned opinion, and shall be final and binding (except that mistakes of law may be appealed to any court in the (name of state) having jurisdiction over the dispute), and judgment may be entered upon it in accordance with applicable law in any court having jurisdiction thereof. The substantially prevailing party in any such arbitration shall be entitled to reasonable attorney's fees and costs from the other party in an amount to be determined by the arbitrator. The substantially prevailing party in any judicial enforcement or review proceeding concerning the arbitration shall also be entitled to reasonable attorney's fees and costs from the other party in an amount to be determined by the court. The provisions of this paragraph shall survive any expiration or termination of this Agreement, but shall not be enforceable in the event of the bankruptcy of a party.

12   Days. If any action is required to be performed, or if any notice, consent or other communication is to be given, on a day that is a Saturday or Sunday or a legal holiday in the jurisdiction in which the action is required to be performed or in which is located the intended recipient of such notice, consent or other communication, such performance shall be deemed to be required, and such notice, consent or other communication shall be deemed to be required to be given, on the first business day following such Saturday, Sunday, or legal holiday. Unless otherwise specified herein, all references herein to a "day" or "days" shall refer to calendar days and not business days.

IN WITNESS WHEREOF, the parties have executed this Agreement as of the day and year set forth below.

SELLER: NAME OF COMPANY

By: _____ (SEAL) _____ Manager

Date of Acceptance: _____

PURCHASER: NAME OF COMPANY

a _____ corporation and/or its assigns

By: _____ (SEAL) Name: _____ Title: _____

   Date of Offer: _____

Exhibit A

Description of Property

Due Diligence for Potential Triple Net Lease Investments

You may be familiar with the term "due diligence" from the purchase or sale of a home or other residential property. Put simply, due diligence is a method of checking a property to evaluate its physical condition so that you can decide whether it's worth the price or not. When done right, due diligence helps you avoid a "money pit," where a considerable amount of your money could be spent in the repair and/or replacement of such expensive items as roofs, furnaces and HVAC systems.

Due diligence serves pretty much the same function in the evaluation of commercial property. It ensures that any land or building the investor buys is in excellent shape, and that it is in line with his or her investment goals. The flip side of the process is to make sure that the investor doesn't buy a "pig in a poke" with hidden structural or environmental problems (leaky roof, outdated plumbing, toxic waste problems, mold, and so forth).

As you can see, commercial property due diligence is more complicated than it is in the residential market. It not only involves the physical inspection of the building but such areas as easements, zoning use, allowed use, encroachments and the like (as described earlier in this book).

In fact, due diligence is even more important in the commercial sector because, unlike the residential market, consumer protection laws generally don't apply here. That's because the law assumes you're fully knowledgeable about commercial properties when you enter into a contract. As such, there aren't as many remedies at your avail in the event of a bad deal. As such, the unbreakable rule is "Caveat emptor!" or "Buyer beware!"

As you might expect, there are many different aspects to the due diligence process, including:

- Tenant profiling

- Highest and best use valuation modeling
- Demographic analysis (employment density, traffic counts, etc.)
- Local economic studies reports
- Municipal tax assessment research
- Comparable property information
- Audit of operating expenses (including taxes, betterments, etc)

In this book, we'll cover with the universal aspects of due diligence, which include tenant profiling, highest and best use valuation modeling, and demographics. We'll focus on these because the other areas tend to be very specific to a property. At the end of this chapter, we'll also provide you with a complete due diligence report so you can see exactly what goes this document.

Tenant Profiling

This is an extremely important task for the simple reason that there must be a good fit between the tenant and the building. For example, putting a pharmacy in a building originally built for, say, an industrial purpose and located away from the general public, would be a fatal mistake. That's because pharmacies are all about health and cleanliness and easy access. Industrial sites, on the other hand, represent the exact opposite of that. Such a mismatch of tenant and property is tantamount to business suicide, both for you and the tenant.

The investment team must profile prospective tenants in depth to ensure that the final selection involves a tenant who's likely to reach maximum potential within the building. It must obey one of the ironclad "laws" of commercial real estate: the market value of a property is measured solely by its worth to the tenant it services.

The range of tenant options spans the local tenant providing a local service and operated by a local one-unit vendor, to a national brand tenant that's a public company and listed on a stock exchange and which has billions of dollars in revenues, and everything in between.

Most national brand tenants can easily be profiled because so much public information is available on them, plus they're rated by respected national agencies such as Moody's, Fitch, and Standard and Poor's. A local tenant can be just as good an investment as a national one; however, you need to evaluate this tenant in a different way since information isn't as readily available. Here's what you (or your investment team) would look for:

A financial history of the tenant, including:

- Financial statements, preferably audited
- Tax returns for the tenant, preferably both the business return and the personal return for the operator
- Sales history for the location

When reviewing the documents:

- You'd want to see an upward trend in all of the numbers.
- You'd need to make sure the sales of the store match up with the income reported.
- You'd want to make sure that the business model actually works for the location. In other words, you don't want to own an ice-making-occupied building in Alaska!

Here are three real-life examples that illustrate the importance of tenant profiling:

Tenant Profile 1: Locally-Owned Restaurant

We recently worked on a transaction where the operators of the location ran a Mexican restaurant in California. They had one store and had been in their location for 40 years. At first glance, this is not very exciting in the business sense because you have to sell a lot of tacos to make good money. Plus, the building was located in a high crime area of the city, was 60 years old and not well maintained. Doesn't sound very appealing as an investment, does it?

However, the operators sold $6 million in tacos every year and had the tax records to prove it. With this sales volume, there was a very low likelihood the business would close its doors.

So, what looked on the surface like a poor investment turned out to actually be a good one – all discovered through thorough tenant profiling.

Tenant Profile 2: National Brand Restaurant

The opposite of the local Mexican restaurant is the national brand tenant with a very specific business model. Sticking with the restaurant example, let's look at McDonald's, which has over 30,000 locations and is listed on the NYSE. The company has been around forever, and is extremely popular with people worldwide.

From an investor's point of view, you can:

- Go online to see how the firm's stock is doing.
- Get detailed reports about the company from analysts all over the world.

Since there's a corporate guarantee, the performance of the company is critical. The sales revenues at a specific McDonald's location are still important because they'll show you if that store is sustainable.

One measure of success (or lack of it) to use for restaurants is the ratio between rent and sales. (Each industry is different for what rent they should pay for a particular store, but restaurants are typically a standard 8%.)

So, the sales-to-rent ratio says that 8% or less of the gross sales of a particular McDonald's restaurant should go to paying the triple net lease rent. According to the ratio, if the store is doing $1 million in sales, then the operator shouldn't pay more than $80,000 in triple net rent per year.

If this operator is paying more that 8%, then he or she may not be able to stay in business very long because the rent is too high. On the other hand, if it's lower, then they should be there a long time.

Typically, the national brand tenants do a good job of projecting the rent for each occupied store. That's because they pursue a tremendous amount of due diligence before they sign a lease, and they have a good idea of the range of the money they'll make for a particular store.

Tenant Profile 3: Regional Medical Service Provider

We were working with "Mr. Sanders," an investor who said he wanted to buy a triple net property within three hours of his home. The criteria were that the lease had to be absolute triple net lease; the lease term had to be 15 years or longer; and the credit had to be "good."

Knowing that everyone has a different definition of "good," we tried to get a better handle on that statement. Did he want an investment-grade tenant that was Standard & Poor's rated, or was a local company okay as long as the sales were strong? Mr. Sanders just kept saying "good."

After several presentations of national brand companies, he decided to purchase a triple net lease investment occupied by a private medical service provider company. The company had about 150 locations, primarily on the East Coast. It provided audited financial statements (AFS) for people to view upon a potential purchase.

The AFS showed that the company had a net worth of about $220 million. Sales were up for the previous three years, and a new CEO had laid out his expansion plans (which allowed for further revenue) recently.

The tenant was no McDonald's in terms of its security as an investment, but Mr. Sanders felt comfortable with the tenant profiling and underwriting because of the amount of third party documentation available.

Additionally, since it wasn't a very popular tenant (in terms of investment), the investor received a higher cap rate and ultimately more money each year. We were comfortable with the transaction since we had a chance to review all of the documents as well.

Highest and Best Use Valuation Modeling

The concept of "highest and best use" states that the value of a property is directly related to the use of that property. In other words, the highest and best use is the reasonably probable use that results in the highest property value. The highest and best use may or may not be the current use of the property. So, the question for any investment team (or investor) is, "How do you determine the highest and best use?"

Although the exact definition of "highest and best use" varies, this use must meet four criteria (in general). These criteria are:

- Legally allowable
- Physically possible
- Financially feasible
- Maximally productive

Let's look at each of these criteria in more detail.

Legally allowable

This area ties in with the concept of zoning discussed earlier. To achieve the highest and best use, only uses that are – or may be – legally allowed by local, state, and/or federal regulations can be considered.

Since buildings last a long time, they may have a use that predates existing zoning regulations. They're considered "legally non-conforming" and are often "grandfathered in," even though they don't meet current zoning regulations.

Physically possible

66

The building must match the site and vice versa. For example, it wouldn't make sense to put a 50,000 square foot warehouse on a 10,000 square foot site. It's not physically possible to do so.

Financial feasibility

The proposed property use must generate adequate revenue to merit the costs of construction, plus a profit for the developer.

When improved property has a proven economic life, financial feasibility has already been established. If, on the other hand, the improved property has a limited remaining economic life, then the question of financial feasibility returns. In other words: How can the investor get maximally productive use of the building and the land?

There are also situations in which the value of the land "as vacant" exceeds the value of the property "as improved." In that case, redevelopment of the site is likely to become the maximally productive use of the property in order for it to remain financially feasible.

Demographic Analysis

This section analyzes potential customers for a Blue Cross/Blue Shield-tenanted building in terms of population and income, typically within a certain radius of the business. This data indicates also indicates trends in terms of population, income and so forth. The following example analyzes the demographics for a 1-, 3-, and 5-mile radius around the business:

Tenant: Blue Cross/Blue Shield

In the identified market area, the current year population is 265,266. In 2000, the Census count in the market area was 251,527. The rate of change since 2000 was 0.58 percent annually. The five-year projection for the population in the market area is 270,249, representing a change of 0.37 percent annually from 2009 to 2014. Currently, the population is 48.0 percent male and 52.0 percent female.

The household count in this market area has changed from 87,780 in 2000 to 92,490 in the current year, a change of 0.57 percent annually. The five-year projection of households is 93,979, a change of 0.32 percent annually from the current year total. Average household size is currently 2.83, compared to 2.83 in the year 2000. The number of families in the current year is 67,152 in the market area.

Housing

Currently, 65.9 percent of the 97,914 housing units in the market area are owner occupied; 28.6 percent are renter occupied; and 5.5 percent are vacant. In 2000, there were 91,219 housing units, 69.2 percent owner occupied, 27.0 percent renter occupied and 3.8 percent vacant. The rate of change in housing units since 2000 is 0.77 percent. Median home value in the market area is $237,902, compared to a median home value of $162,279 for the U.S. In five years, median home value is projected to change by 4.04 percent annually to $290,056. From 2000 to the current year, median home value changed by 5.53 percent annually.

Current median household income is $67,035 in the market area, compared to $54,719 for all U.S. households.

Median household income is projected to be $66,792 in five years. In 2000, median household income was $53,079, compared to $41,811 in 1990. Current average household income is $96,868 in this market area, compared to $71,437 for all U.S. households. Average household income is projected to be $102,073 in five years. In 2000, average household income was $78,201, compared to $56,873 in 1990. Current per capita income is $33,938 in the market area, compared to the U.S. per capita income of $27,277. The per capita income is projected to be $35,682 in five years. In 2000, the per capita income was $27,477, compared to $20,458 in 1990.

Population by Employment

Radius:	1-mile	3-mile	5-mile
Total Businesses	1,164	4,433	14,270
Total Employees	10,937	50,256	130,273

Currently, 92.4 percent of the civilian labor force in the identified market area is employed and 7.6 percent are unemployed. In comparison, 89.4 percent of the U.S. civilian labor force is employed, and 10.6 percent are unemployed. In five years the rate of employment in the market area will be 95.3 percent of the civilian labor force, and unemployment will be 4.7 percent. The percentage of the U.S. civilian labor force that will be employed in five years is 92.9 percent, and 7.1 percent will be unemployed. In 2000, 64.8 percent of the population aged 16 years or older in the market area participated in the labor force, and 0.2 percent were in the Armed Forces.

In the current year, the occupational distribution of the employed population is:

- 73.2 percent in white collar jobs (compared to 61.5 percent of U.S. employment)
- 15.3 percent in service jobs (compared to 17.1 percent of U.S. employment)
- 11.5 percent in blue collar jobs (compared to 21.4 percent of U.S. employment)

In 2000, 78.8 percent of the market area population drove alone to work, and 3.9 percent worked at home. The average travel time to work in 2000 was 32.1 minutes in the market area, compared to the U.S. average of 25.5 minutes.

Population by Education

In 2009, the educational attainment of the population aged 25 years or older in the market area was distributed as follows:

- 10.2 percent had not earned a high school diploma (16.2 percent in the U.S.)
- 21.9 percent were high school graduates only (29.8 percent in the U.S.)
- 10.6 percent had completed an Associate's degree (7.2 percent in the U.S.)
- 25.3 percent had a Bachelor's degree (17.0 percent in the U.S.)
- 15.2 percent had earned a Master's/Professional/Doctorate Degree (9.8 percent in the U.S.)

Summary

As you can see, a lot of work goes into the due diligence process. To give you a better idea of the process we've included a sample field report at the end of this chapter. It was completed for a client on a restaurant location. We recommend that you review the report so you can familiarize yourself with the general format for future reference. Then, continue to the next chapter to get a different field report concerning a specific client and location. Study the report closely to get a standard to use when gauging future field reports.

Sample Due Diligence Report

Mr. Don Johnson
10001 Main Street
Anywhere, USA 00000

December 18, 2009

Re: Tops Restaurant, Anywhere, USA

Dear Don,

Please find the report for your Anywhere, USA, Tops Restaurant site enclosed. This report outlines the main salient facts of the subject property, as well as providing a review of the surrounding marketplace, and detailed demographic reports. Upon review, if you would like additional information regarding this report or the subject property, please do not hesitate to contact me directly anytime at (813) 282-6000.

Yours sincerely,

Broker

Name of Site Services

TOPS RESTAURANT, ANYWHERE, USA

On December 8th and 9th, 2009, Calkain Site Services performed a field report for a freestanding single tenant structure currently leased to Tops Restaurant. This site was located in Anywhere, Monroe County, Utah along the north side of East Stuart Drive (US 221/58) as the southernmost outparcel to a Wal-Mart Supercenter anchored shopping center. Anywhere is a typical tertiary market in southern Utah, with Stuart Drive serving as the main transportation corridor through the area. The immediate marketplace has been canvassed in order to provide a detailed review of the current retail market rental rates, market valuation, as well as identify a proposed best course of action.

PROPERTY CONDITION

1   The property was in excellent condition in relation to the age of the building. All exterior areas were well maintained, landscaping was in order and the parking lot was clean.

2   The interior of the property was in good condition, featuring a clean dining area and bathroom facilities.

3   When I entered the property at approximately 12:30pm, there was good customer traffic, with 8 tables of customers, a relatively full parking lot, and the drive-thru lane was moving at a steady pace.

4   After a review of the market, it is apparent that the subject property constitutes one of the top three retail pad sites within the entire market. This is due to the strength of the other tenants within the surrounding shopping center, as well as the overall access and visibility to the property.

MARKET OVERVIEW

1   The property is located along Stuart Drive (US 221/58), which serves as the main north/south corridor to the area. The property and signage have superior visibility from US 221/58.

2   It is clear that the most recent commercial growth has been along the northern end of Anywhere, and is comprised of the subject property's Wal-Mart shopping center in addition to the Lowe's anchored shopping center just .25 miles north. Existing centers are spread over 2.5 miles to the south and are primarily filled with second and third generation tenants such as Goodwill, Dollar General, and small local and regional tenants.

3   The bulk of national tenants that would be a potential fit for backfilling the subject parcel is currently located as outparcels to the older centers, and have been in their existing locations for quite some time.

COMPARABLE RENTAL RATES

1   Given the tertiary nature of the location, there are very few direct comparable properties, but we have canvassed the entire retail real estate market in Anywhere, UT to provide the most accurate information.

2   The property of best comparison is the vacant Movie Gallery location, which lies as an outparcel to the Tractor Supply/Magic Mart Shopping center. This parcel has been vacant and available for lease for 12 months. The owner is a professional real estate investment firm and they are asking $18/psf on a NNN basis. In discussions with representatives of the owner, they are in preliminary discussions with one of the "major cellular phone carriers," however everything is still preliminary as the tenant is hesitant to move forward with any new location given the current economic situation.

3   The Tractor Supply Shopping center is nearly 90% leased, with Tractor Supply and Magic Mart occupying the majority of the space. This shopping center is the former site of Wal-Mart and Ingles, before Wal-Mart relocated to their new Super Center location. The asking rents for the in-line space is $10-$12/psf, however the representative for the landlord, and institutional owner, indicated they will be very flexible on pricing in order to fill any vacancy if the tenant is viable.

4   Further discussions with the owner's representative on the Tractor Supply shopping center reveal that there is little to no leasing activity present in the Anywhere market. This is caused by the lack of available credit to local franchisees, as well as a general lack of demand for additional retailers.

5   The Kroger-anchored shopping center is an older second or third generation center. While the strength of Kroger still draws traffic into the center, the entire area is aged, including the façade of the building. Local tenants within this center are all discount type concepts, with no national or regional brands. The current landlord is asking $6.00/psf to $8.00/psf in annual rent, depending on the actual tenant, amount of square footage needed, and the general terms of the lease. Even with the low rental rates, there is still vacancy.

GENERAL INFORMATION

1   The subject property

2   Tops Restaurant nationally has average store sales of $967,000 on an annual basis.

3   Quick Service restaurants utilize an industry benchmark of maintaining a rent-to-gross sales ratio of less than 10%, generally preferring to keep that ratio closer to 8% or less.

4   Given the above figures, an average Tops Restaurant would translate into an average rental rate of $96,700/yr ($8,058/mo) to $77,360/yr ($6,446/mo).

5   Higher rental rates may be achieved, but must be justified by higher projected or realized unit level sales.

CONCLUSION

Based upon all of the information collected, there is no immediate demand from a specific group or sector of retail tenants. The relatively small usable size of the parcel and significant costs associated with retrofitting the existing structure for re-use, limit the market value for this site if vacated. The opinion of Calkain Site Services would suggest negotiations with the current tenant to retain an income stream on the property. Additional steps to maximize the benefit to the landlord include:

1   Negotiate with the current tenant in order to retain cash flow. During the negotiations, as compensation for lowered rent, it would be advisable for the landlord to receive a termination clause in the lease if another tenant were to be willing to pay a higher rental amount, potentially offering the current tenant a "right to cure."

2   Additionally, a percentage rent clause should be inserted in the lease in order to ensure any increase in sales will increase the cash flow to the current landlord.

3   If you were to accurately gauge the market for re-tenanting the space, contacting representatives for the existing tenants within the market to gauge an interest would be a logical first step. Of the QSR tenants, the most obvious would be Taco Bell and Burger King. Taco Bell is in a very old structure and might be nearing the end of a previous lease, while Burger King is not currently in the market.

4   It was mentioned by various contacts that the major cellular carriers are actively looking in the Anywhere, UT, market. Generally they utilize a 4,000sf structure, which should be attainable on the subject property, as they do not require a drive-thru lane. It would be advisable to contact their representatives to gauge a general level of interest.

74

Tenant(s):		1. Tops Restaurants
Number of Buildings:		1
Type of Tenant Use:		Quick Service Restaurant with Drive-thru
Approximate number of customers at the time of inspection:		10
Approximate number of cars in the parking lot at time of inspection:		10

General Parking Area

Parking Spaces (approx.): Total # <u>38</u>   Total # Handicap: <u>2</u>

Parking Surface: ☒ Asphalt ☐ Concrete ☐ Other _____

Parking Surface Observation:

Standing Water:	☐ Yes	☒ No
Pot Holes:	☐ Yes	☒ No
Parking Stripes:	☒ Yes	☐ No

Parking Comments:
Parking area is in excellent condition, displaying the tenants proper maintenance and upkeep of the area.

Other Site Features

Curbing:	☒ Concrete	☐ Extruded Asphalt	☐ Other _____
Sidewalks:		☒ Concrete	☐ Other _____
Fencing:		☒ Chain link	☐ Other _____
Irrigation System:		☒ Yes	☐ No

Landscaping:
Landscaping consists of small shrubs and mulch ground cover surrounding the building with grass to the front of the property. The south and western borders of the property have concrete retaining walls.

Signs

☒ **Building Mounted**   ☒ Pylon sign
☒ **At Entrance**   ☐ Other:

Comments

Are there any identified issues or concerns regarding the site? Please describe: Site and surrounding area are in excellent condition and show signs of tenant taking care of the property with no deferred maintenance.

Overall Condition of Site? ☒ Excellent ☐ Good ☐ Fair ☐ Poor

75

Building Exterior

How many floors? 1
How many means ingress/egress? _____

Is there a: ☐ Balcony   ☐ Terrace

Are there any exterior awnings?   ☐ Yes   ☒ No

Roof: ☒ Flat   ☐ Sloped

Exterior roof ladder for access?   ☐ Yes   ☒ No

Exterior Walls & Superstructure:
    ☒ Brick   ☐ Plaster   ☐ Wood Siding   ☐ Metal   ☐ Stone   ☐ Other _____

Foundation: ☐ Excavated   ☒ Slab-on-grade   ☐ Unknown

Comments

Is there any damage or cracks to the exterior façade?
Please describe: Exterior of building is in excellent condition with no signs of deferred maintenance or excessive wear and tear.

Overall Condition of Site?   ☒ Excellent   ☐ Good   ☐ Fair   ☐ Poor

Building Interior

Floor Finish: ☐ Carpet   ☒ Tile   ☐ Unfinished   ☐ Other:_____

Floor Structure: ☒ Concrete Slab   ☐ Wood sub-floor   ☐ Unknown

Window Type: ☐ Single-glazed   ☒ Double-glazed   ☐ Other _____

Wall Finish:
☒ Sheetrock/Plaster   ☐ Tile   ☐ Wood Panels   ☒ Wallpaper   ☐ Painted   ☐ Other _____

Ceiling: ☐ Sheetrock   ☒ Tile Ceiling   ☐ 2 x 4   ☒ 2 x 2   ☐ Other _____

Bathrooms: # Men's _____   # Woman's _____   # Unisex _____

Typical Men's room: # urinals _____ # toilets _____ # handicapped stalls _____ # sinks _____

Comments

Is there any identified damage to the interior (please note any ceiling stains)?
Please describe: Interior of facility was in excellent condition with no signs of excessive wear and tear.

Overall Condition of interior: ☐ Excellent   ☒ Good   ☐ Fair   ☐ Poor

Traffic Patterns

Is the subject property located on a US Route?   ☒ Yes   ☐ No

Is the subject property located on a State Route?   ☐ Yes   ☒ No

What is the approximate distance to the closest Interstate?   Distance:_____   Interstate #: _____

Is the subject property located on a hard corner?   ☐ Yes   ☒ No

How many lanes is the road at primary street? ☐ Two ☒ Four ☐ Other _____

Traffic flow on road at primary entry:

☐ Heavy ☒ Moderate ☐ Light Time of Day:_____

Are there any turning restrictions for entering the site from the primary street? ☐ Yes ☒ No

If yes, please describe: _____

Are there any turn restrictions for exiting the site to the primary street? ☐ Yes ☒ No

If yes, please describe: _____

Is there a traffic signal at the primary entry into the site? ☒ Yes ☐ No

If not, please describe location of the closest traffic signal (include direction & approximate distance from primary entry): _____

Are there any turning restrictions for entering the site to the secondary street? ☐ Yes ☒ No

If yes, please describe: _____

Are there any turn restrictions for exiting the site to the secondary street? ☐ Yes ☒ No

If yes, please describe: _____

Is there a traffic signal at the secondary entry into the site? ☐ Yes ☒ No

Is the subject property part of a shopping center? ☒ Yes ☐ No

If yes, describe: The subject property is an outparcel to a Wal-Mart Supercenter anchored shopping center.

Is the subject property located in an area containing similar use properties? ☒ Yes ☐ No

What types of properties are located directly to the North of the subject property?

☒ Retail
☐ Fast Food/Restaurants
☐ Office
☐ Gas/Convenience Store
☐ Industrial
☐ Residential
☐ Other: _____

What type of properties are directly located to the South of the subject property?

☒ Retail
☐ Fast Food/Restaurants
☐ Office
☐ Gas/Convenience Store
☐ Industrial
☐ Residential
☐ Other: _____

What types of properties are located directly to the East of the subject property?

☒ Retail
☐ Fast Food/Restaurants
☐ Office
☐ Gas/Convenience Store
☐ Industrial
☐ Residential
☐ Other: _____

What type of properties are directly located to the West of the subject property?

☒ Retail
☐ Fast Food/Restaurants
☐ Office
☐ Gas/Convenience Store
☐ Industrial
☐ Residential
☐ Other: _____

Sample of a Due Diligence Report for a Triple Net Lease Investment

Because the field report is the heart and soul of due diligence, we thought it appropriate to devote an entire chapter to it. Obviously, it's important to read the report information carefully since it will alert you to both the advantages and potential advantages of a property.

As you'll see, the field report in this chapter concerns a freestanding, single tenant structure that, at the time of the report, was leased to a tenant in Durham, N.C. However, such a location could be found anywhere in the U.S.

The report is a standard form used by our firm. Other brokers will have similar forms, differing only in the particulars.

After the table of contents, you'll find a cover letter detailing such information as:

- History of Durham
- Retail Development
- Competition
- Stability
- Growth
- Barriers to Entry

The cover letter contains both personal and objective information gathered by the broker. It gives you the necessary details about a particular property and its location.

The actual field report form following the cover letter presents a mostly objective view of the particular property in terms of the physical condition of the building (interior and exterior), the parking lot, surrounding neighborhood, etc.

The Cell Store – Durham, NC

Table of Contents

On May 29 and 30, 2008, Calkain Site Services performed a field report for a freestanding, single tenant structure currently leased to The Cell Store. This site was located in the city of Durham, Durham County N.C. It is situated as an out parcel to a large regional shopping center known as Franklin Square, located adjacent to State Road 74, which serves as the main East/West Corridor for the surrounding trade area. In order to provide local knowledge of the area and potential future developments, I met with Mr. John Wilson of the Durham County Economic Development Commission. Mr. Wilson serves as the Project Administrator, and is a native resident of Durham County. The following topics were discussed, and highlights have been provided:

HISTORY OF DURHAM

1   Durham was originally supported by the textile industry, however as the sustainability of that trade has waivered, the area has shifted its concentration to high technology facilities.

2   Currently Durham serves as a bedroom community to Charlotte, situated only 20 minutes from the CBD.

3   Historic Durham is located approximately five miles to the west of the subject property. This area is filled with second-generation facilities and local light industrial uses.

RETAIL DEVELOPMENT

1   Franklin Square – (location of subject property) – anchored by Home Depot, Kohl's, Wal-Mart, Lowe's, and many other national retailers.

2   Durham Mall – formerly one of the oldest enclosed malls, Durham mall is currently under construction, with the current owner converting it to an open-air mall, complete with Harris Teeter and potentially Super Target as the main anchors.

3   Eastridge Mall – Owned by Westfield, Eastridge mall is slightly dated, however still hosts substantial anchor tenants Dillard's, JC Penny, Belk, and Sears.

4   There is an existing Target center located south of the Eastridge Mall. While no solid proof has been provided, it is rumored that Target is going to shutter this location in favor of relocating to the Durham Mall redevelopment project.

5   There's a variety of small retail developments along Franklin Blvd between New Hope road on the west and South Main St. on the east.

COMPETITION

1   The Cell Store has a distinct advantage over the other wireless carriers with the use of this freestanding location.

2   The grade of the subject property sits substantially above road grade, providing excellent visibility for passing traffic.

STABILITY

1   The Franklin Square development has been an example of retail success for over a decade. While occupancy remains extremely high, asking rents for inline space ranges from $20psf to $28psf, on a NNN basis depending on location and size of the space.

2   A specific example of the retail success is Sam's Club; the location in Franklin Square has been expanded twice to meet the needs of the high traffic and high sales volume. This expansion has been preferred over relocation to a newer facility, as the target location is superior to any available land.

GROWTH

1   Residential growth has continued throughout the south and eastern portions of Durham County, while the northern and western regions are predominately rural.

2   As the greater Charlotte area continues to grow, first time homebuyers have selected Durham as a lower cost alternative, while offering a high quality of living.

BARRIERS TO ENTRY

1   There is vacant land located along the south side of Franklin Blvd, directly south of Franklin Square. This land abuts a residential community that has prevented any commercial development for over 15 years. Consequently the land has been changed to residential use in the future land use map of Durham County.

2   The only potential large new commercial development site exists directly north of Franklin Square, along the northern border of Interstate 85. This site was originally planned to connect with the Franklin Square development via an Interstate overpass located between the Kohl's and Lowe's anchored sections of the existing shopping center. This option is unlikely to come to fruition based upon the significant cost and regulation of the interstate system.

Tenant(s): The Cell Store
Number of Buildings: 1
Type of Tenant Use: Free Standing Cellular telephone retail store
Approximate number of customers at the time of inspection: 15
Approximate number of cars in the parking lot at time of inspection: 9

General Parking Area

Parking Spaces (approx.):   Total # 32   Total # Handicap: 2

Parking Surface: ☒Asphalt   ☐Concrete   ☐Other _____

Parking Surface Observation:

Standing Water	☐ Yes	☒ No
Pot Holes:	☐ Yes	☒ No
Parking Stripes:	☒ Yes	☐ No

Parking Comments:
Parking area in excellent condition with no apparent damage and limited amount of visual wear.

Utilities

Site Utilities: ☒ Municipal Water   ☒ Municipal Sewer   ☒ Gas   ☐ Oil

Other Site Features

Curbing: ☒ Concrete   ☐ Extruded Asphalt   ☐Other _____

Sidewalks: ☒ Concrete   ☐ Other _____

Irrigation System: ☒ Yes   ☐ No

Landscaping (describe): The site was surrounded by small shrubs with pine straw as ground cover. Trees were spaced throughout the perimeter, with grass along the eastern side of the property.

Drainage System (describe): Surface drains were located along the curb system at both east and west portions of the parking area, along the southern border of the parking surface.

Dumpster Location: Dumpster is located in the rear of the building (north side) and is enclosed within a brick area.

Dumpster Details:

Screened	☒ Yes	☐ No
Recycle Bins	☐ Yes	☒ No
Noticeable Odors	☐ Yes	☒ No

Signs

☒ Building Mounted   ☒ At Entrance   ☒ Pylon Sign   ☐ Other

Lighting

☒ Pole mounted #_5__   ☒ Building mounted #_29_   ☐ Other _____

Comments

Are there any identified issues or concerns regarding the site?
Please describe: No, the site is in excellent condition, and has wonderful visibility from both the interior of the shopping center as well as from Franklin Blvd. Parking area, building, and landscaping are all in wonderful condition.

Overall Condition of Site?   ☒ Excellent   ☐ Good   ☐ Fair   ☐ Poor

Building Exterior

How many floors? 1   **How many means ingress/egress?** 2

Roof: ☒ Flat   ☐ Sloped
Exterior roof ladder for access?   ☒ Yes   ☐ No

Roof Type:
☐ Built-up   ☐ Rubber membrane   ☐ Wooden Shingle   ☐ Asphalt Shingle
☐ Pre-formed Metal   ☒ Unknown   ☐ Other _____

Exterior Walls & Superstructure:
☒ Brick   ☒ Stucco   ☐ Wood Siding   ☐ Metal   ☒ Stone   ☐ Other _____

Foundation: ☐ Excavated   ☒ Slab-on-grade   ☐ Unknown

Is there any damage or cracks to the exterior façade?
Please describe: No, Exterior of building in excellent condition

Overall Condition of Site?   ☒ Excellent   ☐ Good   ☐ Fair   ☐ Poor

Building Interior

Floor Finish: ☒ Carpet   ☐ Tile   ☒ Wood   ☐ Other:_____

Floor Structure: ☒ Concrete Slab   ☐ Wood sub-floor   ☐ Unknown

Window Type: ☐ Single-glazed   ☒ Double-glazed   ☐ Other _____

Wall Finish:
☒ Sheetrock/Plaster   ☐ Til   ☒ Wood Panels   ☐ Wallpaper   ☐ Painted   ☐ Other _____

Ceiling: ☐ Sheetrock   ☒ Tile Ceiling   ☐ 2 x 4   ☒ 2 x 2   ☐ Other _____

Fire Protection System: **HVAC System:**
☒ Sprinkler   ☐ Chiller
☒ Alarm   ☐ Furnace
☒ Smoke Detectors   ☒ Roof-top package
☒ Portable fire extinguishers   ☐ Heat pump (individual)
☐ Unknown

82

Comments

Is there any identified damage to the interior (please note any ceiling stains)? Please describe:
<u>No, interior of building was in excellent condition</u>

Overall Condition of interior: ☒ Excellent   ☐ Good   ☐ Fair   ☐ Poor

Project Accessibility

Is handicapped parking available?	☒ Yes	☐ No
Are handicapped spaces well marked?	☒ Yes	☐ No
Is the main entrance doorway wide enough for a wheel chair?	☒ Yes	☐ No
Are the common interior areas accessible to the handicapped?	☒ Yes	☐ No

Traffic Patterns

Is the subject property located on a US Route?   ☐ Yes   ☒ No

Is the subject property located on a State Route?   ☒ Yes   ☐ No

What is the approximate distance to the closest Interstate?   Distance:_____   Interstate #: _____

Is the subject property located on a hard corner?   ☐ Yes   ☒ No

How many curb cuts on the primary street?   ☒ One   ☐ Two

How many lanes is the road at primary street?   ☐ Two   ☐ Four   ☒ Six

Traffic flow on road at primary entry: ☒ Heavy   ☐ Moderate   ☐ Light

Time of Day:_____

How many curb cuts on the secondary street?   ☒ One   ☐ Two

How many lanes is the road at secondary street?   ☒ Two   ☐ Four   ☐ Other _____

Traffic flow on road at secondary entry: ☐ Heavy   ☒ Moderate   ☐ Light

Time of Day:_____

Are there any turning restrictions for entering the site from the primary street?   ☐ Yes   ☒ No

   If yes, please describe:
<u>No, access is available for both east and westbound traffic</u>

Are there any turn restrictions for exiting the site to the primary street?   ☐ Yes   ☒ No

   If yes, please describe: _____

Is there a traffic signal at the primary entry into the site?   ☒ Yes   ☐No

   If not, please describe location of the closest traffic signal (include direction & approximate distance from primary entry): _____

Are there any turning restrictions for entering the site to the secondary street?   ☒ Yes   ☐No

   If yes, please describe: _____

Are there any turn restrictions for exiting the site to the secondary street?   ☒ Yes   ☐No

   If yes, please describe: _____

Is there a traffic signal at the secondary entry into the site?   ☐ Yes   ☒No

If not, please describe location of the closest traffic signal (include direction & approximate distance from primary entry): _____

Is the subject property part of a shopping center?   ☒ Yes   ☐No

If yes, describe:

Is the subject property located in an area containing similar use properties   ☒ Yes   ☐No

What type of properties are located directly to the North of the subject property?

☒ Retail
☐ Fast Food/Restaurants
☐ Office
☐ Gas/Convenience Store
☐ Industrial
☐ Residential
☐ Other: _____

What type of properties are directly located to the South of the subject property?

☐ Retail
☐ Fast Food/Restaurants
☐ Office
☐ Gas/Convenience Store
☐ Industrial
☐ Residential
☒ Other: _____

What types of properties are located directly to the East of the subject property?

☒ Retail
☐ Fast Food/Restaurants
☐ Office
☐ Gas/Convenience Store
☐ Industrial
☐ Residential
☐ Other: _____

What type of properties are directly located to the West of the subject property?

☐ Retail
☐ Fast Food/Restaurants
☐ Office
☐ Gas/Convenience Store
☐ Industrial
☐ Residential
☐ Other: _____

Characteristics of the Surrounding Neighborhoods

North

One Mile	*Three Mile*	*Five Miles*
☒ Retail	☒ Retail	☒ Retail
☐ Office	☒ Office	☒ Office
☐ Fast Food/Restaurants	☐ Fast Food/Restaurants	☐ Fast Food/Restaurants
☐ Gas/Convenience Store	☐ Gas/Convenience Store	☒ Gas/Convenience Store
☐ Industrial	☐ Industrial	☐ Industrial
☐ Residential	☒ Residential	☒ Residential
☐ Other: _____	☒ Other: _____	☒ Other: _____
Major Projects:_____	Major Projects:_____	Major Projects: _____
Wal-Mart	Durham Hospital	Mostly rural residential

South

One Mile	*Three Miles*	*Five Miles*
☐ Retail	☐ Retail	☐ Retail
☐ Office	☐ Office	☐ Office
☐ Fast Food/Restaurants	☐ Fast Food/Restaurants	☐ Fast Food/Restaurants

☐ Gas/Convenience Store
☐ Industrial
☒ Residential
☐ Other: _____
Major Projects:
Mostly residential

☐ Gas/Convenience Store
☐ Industrial
☒ Residential
☐ Other: _____
Major Projects:
Mostly residential

☐ Gas/Convenience Store
☐ Industrial
☒ Residential
☐ Other: _____
Major Projects:
Mostly residential

East

One Mile
☒ Retail
☐ Office
☐ Fast Food/Restaurants
☐ Gas/Convenience Store
☐ Industrial
☐ Residential
☐ Other: _____
Major Projects:
Lowe's
Kohl's
HH Gregg

Three Miles
☒ Retail
☐ Office
☒ Fast Food/Restaurants
☒ Gas/Convenience Store
☐ Industrial
☐ Residential
☐ Other: _____
Major Projects:_____

Five Miles
☒ Retail
☒ Office
☒ Fast Food/Restaurants
☒ Gas/Convenience Store
☐ Industrial
☒ Residential
☐ Other:
Major Projects: _____

West

One Mile
☒ Retail
☐ Office
☒ Fast Food/Restaurants
☒ Gas/Convenience Store
☐ Industrial
☐ Residential
☐ Other: _____
Major Projects:_____
Home Depot
Durham Mall
Northgate Mall

Three Miles
☒ Retail
☐ Office
☒ Fast Food/Restaurants
☒ Gas/Convenience Store
☐ Industrial
☒ Residential
☐ Other: _____
Major Projects:_____
Historic Downtown
Local tenants

Five Miles
☒ Retail
☒ Office
☒ Fast Food/Restaurants
☒ Gas/Convenience Store
☒ Industrial
☒ Residential
☐ Other: _____
Major Projects: _____
Mostly residential

Categories of Triple-Net Lease Investment Property Sellers

There are many different buyers of triple-net lease investment properties, but sellers generally fall into one of three categories:

- Investors/owners of leased properties
- Owner/user
- Build-to-suit developers

Investors/Owners of Leased Properties

In this category, there will typically be a restricted amount of time left on the triple-net lease agreement. In many cases, this necessitates either re-leasing or a series of short-term options.

For all practical purposes, an investor/owner is a known quantity in terms of analysis by an investment team. In other words, the team has a business history to go by. It can analyze the base rent, review the expense payment history, and, in some cases, be able to evaluate the sales volume history in order to determine the potential for future income.

Owner/Users of Leased Properties

The triple-net lease is well suited to sale/leasebacks. If you're not familiar with this concept, it means that the property owner/user sells that property and then simultaneously leases it back from the buyer. In these situations, the seller goes from being the owner/user to being a "lessee" or tenant.

Here's an example of how a sales-leaseback works: XYZ Motor Company has an asset(s) that it currently owns outright and operates out of. It's a 100,000 sq. ft. building in which the firm's popular hybrid vehicle models are assembled. The company knows it will be in this particular building for a long time. However, its financial team has determined that owning all of this real estate doesn't make the company any immediate income or help the cash flow situation.

So the company signs a 20-year triple net lease, and the building is sold for $10 million with a lease payment of $800,000 year. XYZ controls expenses of building (utilities, taxes, maintenance, etc.) and, as sole tenant, keeps operating as normal.

So the investor is going to get a nice eight percent return with potential incremental increases, but what's in it for XYZ Motor Company? Well, it was able to pay off the mortgage on the building and can now write off the entire lease payment (which is considered an operating expense). So, as a result of the sales-leaseback agreement, XYZ got a big chunk of money, paid down debt, and received a tax benefit.

Depending on the company and the situation, there are number of other objectives a seller might want to achieve, such as:

- Finance operational growth and investment. (For example, they can build new facilities, buy new equipment, reallocate capital, invest in new technology, and so forth.)
- Restructure the management of the company
- Buy back company stock

Through achievement of these objectives, owner/users can realize a considerable number of benefits. They can:

- Monetize the real estate
- Obtain 100% fair market value of the asset
- Improve working capital
- Convert illiquid assets into cash
- Quickly consummate transactions
- Improve the company balance sheet
- Avoid the risks of real estate ownership
- Gain tax advantages

- Be able to write off the entire lease payment as an operating expense as opposed to only the interest on the loan payments or depreciation over 39 years (the standard timeframe that a commercial building is depreciated)
- Enhance financial liquidity
- Have the lease terms and conditions tailored to meet their needs

The final point is beneficial for both sellers and buyers. The two parties can negotiate an agreement that meets specific needs for certain situations. For example, an investor may want a higher purchase price in exchange for pre-determined rent increases as opposed to assuming the risk of cost-of-living increases.

Or the investor may want to trade a short initial lease term for a series of 10-year options rather than five-year options. And let's not forget the tenants; they'll likely feel comfortable with the obligations of a bond-type lease because they already know the property.

Your investment team should be aware of one potential downside that concerns the physical plant rather than the lease itself. Sometimes, owner/users over-improve their buildings in order to burnish their company's image. There's nothing wrong with that, of course, until they expect the buyer to pay for over-market improvements. So, your investment team should be alert to such over-improvements in terms of their evaluation of properties.

Build-to-Suit Developers

It's usually easier and simpler for your investment team to evaluate these types of properties since the developers will have all the necessary information available for evaluation.

A developer's top objective is to build. With a lease in hand, he or she can obtain construction financing and create the homes, buildings, and other structures.

The developer's second goal is to generate a profit through sales. He or she will build a return into the transaction. However, depending on the size and nature of the development, costs for the developer may be comparatively low because of economies of scale in generating a large volume of product.

One of the benefits of dealing with developers is that the lease is already drawn up. The investment team's thorough analysis of that document's terms virtually eliminates the chance of unwelcome contractual surprises for you.

There are also disadvantages to these types of deals. With developers, there's usually no site history, so you may not know how well the investment will perform. To work around this gap, your investment team will need to do some close analysis of the situation before making a decision. A second potential pitfall occurs when the developers accede to a demanding tenant, even when the terms may hurt the property's investment value.

Now let's move on to another form of investment for triple-net leases – real estate investment trusts.

REITS as Triple Net Lease Investment Vehicles

If you don't want the responsibility of maintaining triple net leases with one or more clients, you might consider real estate investment trusts (REITs), which can be a good source for triple net lease investments. REITs typically buy properties such as office buildings, manufacturing facilities, retail stores, and restaurant franchises, and then do a sales-leaseback with the former owners.

REITs are corporations or trusts that use the pooled capital of many investors to purchase and manage income property. Just like stocks, REITs are traded on major exchanges.

Generally speaking, REITs are divided into two categories:

- Public REITS – as the name suggests, they're traded on open exchanges. This makes it easy to enter and exit such funds.
- Private REITs – these funds are "closed," which makes them harder to enter and exit. However, one advantage is that these funds are not as subject to daily market fluctuations as are public REITs.

So, why would an investor buy into a REIT as opposed to other investments? There are several benefits to doing so. First, REITs receive special tax considerations. In order to qualify as a REIT for tax purposes, a company must return a specified percentage of earnings to its shareholders in the form of dividends.

Unlike traditional real estate investments, REITs must also provide a highly liquid method of investing in real estate, and easy liquidity. Plus, as a shareholder, you can receive value in the form of both dividend income and the appreciation of share value.

Private REITs also aren't as highly correlated with the major indices as most industries are. This can help maintain your overall returns, especially during market downturns.

Finally, REITs own "hard" physical assets such as land and buildings, and they often sign their tenants to long-term lease contracts. Due to these factors, any REIT chosen will tend to be very stable in terms of investment and income.

There are also downsides to investing REITs. A potential disadvantage is poor management, which can lead to inferior performance or losses. Obviously, due diligence on the management is necessary before you ever invest in a particular fund.

A second potential disadvantage lies in the fact that REITs can only reinvest up to 10 percent of their annual profits back into their core business lines. As a result, many REITs grow at slower pace than the average Wall Street stock. Thus, the average (publicly-traded) REIT posts annual earnings growth lower than that of, say, the Standard & Poor's 500.

Be aware that while the REIT business tends to be a fairly stable one, these investments are not without risk. For example, their dividend payments are not guaranteed, and the real estate market is prone to cyclical downturns.

REIT Classifications

Now, let's look at the general classifications of REITS in terms of real estate and triple-net lease investments.

Equity REITs

These funds invest in and own properties (hence the name, "equity"). They're responsible for the value of their real estate assets, with revenues derived primarily from their properties' rents.

Mortgage REITs

As the name suggests, these funds deal in the investment in and ownership of property mortgages. These REITs loan money for mortgages to real estate owners, or they buy existing mortgages or mortgage-backed securities. Their revenues come primarily from the interest they earn on mortgage loans.

Hybrid REITs

Hybrids combine the investment strategies of equity REITs and mortgage REITs by investing in both properties and mortgages.

When picking REITs, your investment team will look at the fundamentals of each specific trust. These fundamentals are pretty much the same as you find in other equity investments (solid track records, a professional and effective management team, reasonable valuations, and good prospects for growth). More specifically, your team should look at the following areas in relation to REITs:

- Geographic Diversification. It's usually wise to focus on large and broadly diversified companies (rather than smaller ones) because they have less exposure to regional economic weakness, natural disasters, and so forth.
- Current Dividend Yields. When investing in REITs, our advice is to look for stocks that pay above-average annual yields.
- Long-Term Dividend Growth. Look for REITs with long track records of consistent and growing dividends.
- Dividend Payout Ratios. Calculate this ration by taking a firm's annual dividend payment per share and dividing that figure by its EPS (earnings per share). The resultant number is a measure of the percentage of its earnings a REIT pays out in the form of dividends. Because REITs are required to pay out a specified high percentage of their earnings in the form of dividends, many of these firms carry a relatively high payout ratio. Occasionally, however, a company may pay out over 100 percent of current earnings in the form of dividends. As you might expect, this type of payout ratio is unsustainable over the long term, and many of these firms are eventually forced to lower their dividends. When searching for high-quality REITs, experts advise that you look for companies with payout ratios below 100 percent.

- Availability of a Dividend Reinvestment Plan (DRIP). Analyze each REIT to see whether or not it offers a DRIP. This is an important feature because a DRIP plan minimizes or eliminates transaction fees you'd otherwise have to pay in order to reinvest your dividend payments back into the underlying stock. Be sure to avoid this common mistake made by many REIT investors: focusing solely on dividend yields. High yields are great, of course, but corporate dividends are not guaranteed. You could be setting yourself up for disappointment if you don't analyze the overall quality of a REIT.

So you have the lowdown on REITs and where they might fit into your investment portfolio. In the next chapter, we'll turn our attention to one of the best wealth-building and tax-deferring tools at your disposal – the Tax-Deferred 1031-1033 Exchange Law.

The Tax Deferred 1031-1033 Exchange Code

As a commercial real estate investor, you have valuable tax mechanisms at your avail. Known as 1031 and 1033 Exchanges, these tools allows you to defer your taxes and build wealth over time. They are a popular choice for clients who have land that produces little or no income, or for those who have a management-intensive building (shopping center, apartment complex, and so on) and who want a property with fewer hassles.

Before we into how the 1031 can help you achieve those benefits, we want to give you a primer on capital gains in the United States, just in case you're not familiar with the topic. In America, individuals and corporations are required to pay income tax on the net total of all their capital gains, just like they do on other types of income. Capital gains are generally taxed at a preferential rate in comparison to ordinary income. This provides incentives for investors to make capital investments and to fund entrepreneurial activity.

How much you, as an investor, are taxed depends on both your tax bracket, and the amount of time your investment was held before you sold it. Generally speaking, capital gains are taxed on a short-term or long-term basis, as follows:

- Short-term capital gains are taxed at the ordinary income tax rate, and are defined as investments held for a year or less before being sold.
- Long-term capital gains apply to assets held for more than one year. They're taxed at a lower rate than short-term gains. This rate is currently zero percent for taxpayers in the 10 percent and 15 percent tax brackets, and 15 percent for taxpayers in the 25 percent, 28 percent, 33 percent, and 35 percent tax brackets.

These reduced tax rates were passed with a sunset provision and are effective through 2010; if they're not extended before that time, they'll expire and revert to the rates in effect before 2003 (generally 20 percent).

As a result of the Tax Reconciliation Act signed into law by President George W. Bush on May 17, 2006, the reduced 15 percent tax rate on qualified dividends and long-term capital gains, previously scheduled to expire in 2008, was extended through 2010. The following changes were specified in the act:

- In 2010, the tax rate on qualified dividends and long-term capital gains is zero percent for those in the 10 percent and 15 percent income tax brackets.
- After 2010, dividends will be taxed at the taxpayer's ordinary income tax rate, regardless of his or her tax bracket.
- After 2010, the long-term capital gains tax rate will increase unless the president signs new legislation.

Down to Business

Now let's look at how 1031 and 1033 Tax Deferred Exchange law works in terms of real estate and, of course, triple net lease investments.

Normally, when a property is sold and a profit is earned ("capital gain") from that sale, the government wants its share through a tax on that profit ("capital gains tax"). However, through application of the 1031-1033* federal law, you can sell one property and buy another without incurring capital gains taxes. The only requirement is that you have to reinvest all your profits into the next property (or properties) within a specific timeline.

*The 1033 section of the law refers to the "involuntary conversion" of the property "as a result of its destruction in whole or in part, due to theft, seizure, or requisition or condemnation or threat or imminence thereof." Often, in this situation, a government entity (local, state or federal), takes a property by condemnation or eminent domain, and it has the opportunity to exchange into a property without paying capital gains taxes. Each entity has their own specifics on parameters and timing.

The rules for a 1033 are different from a 1031. For example, no qualified intermediary is required because the owners are allowed to hold the proceeds themselves. They also have more time (two years) to buy a replacement property and defer capital gains tax. The government allows more latitude because it wasn't the owner's decision to sell the property. This rule also allows the owner to earn interest on the money during the two-year time period.

Here's an example of how the 1031 Tax Deferred Exchange could work for you:

Assume you buy an investment property for $1 million. After a few years, it appreciates to $1.25 million and you decide to sell for a nice $250,000 profit. However, assuming a tax rate of 15 percent, you owe the government $37,500 on that gain. Needless to say, you'd prefer not to pay that money at this time. So, instead of taking the money, you invest that $1.25 million into another property, and you don't have to pay any taxes on the capital gain at that time.

Because the 1031 Exchange is a government program, there are specific rules and regulations to follow in order to qualify for a 1031 Tax Deferred Exchange. Here they are:

- The property must be held for investment purposes or used in your trade or business ("qualifying property").
- The exchange must be "like-kind" (e.g., investment property exchanged for investment property, a duplex exchanged for a net lease investment, etc.).
- The like-kind property must be identified within 45 days of the closing on the initial property.
- The closing on the second property must take place within 180 days following the close on the first property.
- The properties to be exchanged must be located in the United States.
- An exchange must be made that's equal to or greater in both value and equity. Any cash or debt relief received above this amount is considered "boot" and is taxable.
- All proceeds from the initial sale must be turned over to a "qualified intermediary" (the person or company acting as the "middleman"). The qualified intermediary holds the funds from the first property in escrow until

the closing on the second property occurs. The intermediary also assists you with paperwork preparation and other services to ensure the transaction goes as smoothly as possible. Note: It's important to remember that any of your proceeds not under control of the intermediary are subject to taxation.

- Your personal residence can't be exchanged for income property, and income or investment property cannot be exchanged for a personal residence in which you reside.

Types of Exchanges

The most common type of 1031 Exchange is the deferred exchange. The term "deferred" refers to the fact that the sale of the relinquished property and the purchase of the replacement property can occur at different times.

There are three other types of 1031 Exchanges. There's the simple (relatively speaking) straight exchange in which two parties trade properties of equal or approximate value. And then there's the complex multi-party exchange in which three or more parties buy, sell, or exchange properties.

There's also the reverse exchange, also called a Title-Holding Exchange. This is an exchange in which the replacement property is purchased and closed on before the relinquished property is sold. It's basically a method of paying yourself back and incurring zero out of pocket costs.

Usually, a qualified intermediary (QI) takes title to the replacement property and holds title until the taxpayer can find a buyer for his or her relinquished property and close on the sale under an Exchange Agreement with the intermediary. Following the closing of the relinquished property (or simultaneous with this closing), the QI conveys title to the replacement property to the taxpayer.

The advantage of this exchange is that you're sure to have the replacement property in your possession. The risk is that you have to identify the property within 45 days and completing the acquisition within the 180-day limitation. To help with reverse exchanges, the IRS issued a "revenue procedure" that established the notion of an Exchange Accommodation Title-holder (EAT). This is just another name for a qualified intermediary. The EAT buys the replacement property using money that you advanced. He or she then holds the property for you. After that, you have the 180-day replacement period to find a buyer for the property that you desire to relinquish.

The 1031 as a Wealth Builder

Earlier, we stated the 1031 exchange is a great way to build wealth. Now, let's get more specific as to why this is so. We've already mentioned that you can transfer equity to a new property and defer taxes, but this is where it gets good: As part of the exchange, you can buy a new and larger property, thus growing income and appreciation. Plus, you can make as many exchanges as you want under the law and keep on deferring taxes and getting more income and more appreciation.

For example, you may be an investor selling your business, land, or other investment that requires intensive management (apartments, multi-tenant office buildings, and so forth). Maybe you're retiring, or perhaps you don't want the management headaches anymore. If that were the case, then you'd likely be looking for a 1031 replacement property with few or no requirements for maintenance. Therefore, single tenant triple-net lease properties are ideal candidates for you and 1031 property exchanges.

Why the Services of a Broker Are Crucial for a 1031 Exchange

Under 1031 rules, an investor has 45 days in which to find a replacement property. The IRS established this time frame in order to get money quickly back into the economy. At first glance, it may seem like a reasonable amount of time, but it's not. When dealing with complicated real estate and triple net lease transactions, it can be excruciatingly short. In fact, it can be a time of high anxiety if an investor doesn't prepare properly for the process.

Therefore, to reduce the anxiety and avoid the capital gains tax, we recommend that our clients start considering a 1031 exchange before they even put their property on the market. Here's a real-life example to illustrate our point:

Mr. and Mrs. "Johnson" came into a windfall. They sold a piece of citrus-producing land to building developers for $3 million in cash. Obviously, they didn't want to pay capital gains on this large amount of money, so they started out to find exchange assets by themselves. Unfortunately, not only did the Johnsons find the whole process complicated and time consuming, but they also had a hard time identifying the assets they were looking for. They knew they wanted approximately an 8 percent return but nothing was fitting the bill.

Before they knew it, the Johnsons were down to the last week of the 45-day period. They'd identified three properties but had no letters of intent or control of any of them. Finally, they selected a bank property (with only a 6 percent return) and got it under contract.

However, once they got into the due diligence phase, environmental issues were discovered, and their attorney advised them not to buy the property. The net result was that the Johnsons were left with zero options and had to pay a hefty capital gains tax.

As you can see, the Johnsons would have been better served by working with a broker before their land transaction was completed. That broker would then have had a fiduciary responsibility to select properties with fully identified contracts for each of them, and the Johnsons would have had time to objectively pick a property that best met their investment needs and complete due diligence on that property in order to make sure the final investment was a sound one.

Summary

As you've learned in this chapter, the 1031 and 1033 Tax-Deferred Exchange Code is a great vehicle for making the most of your money. Now, it's time to move on to another area of triple net leases in which you can plan for the future – zero cash flow transactions.

Zero Cash Flow Transactions

On the surface, you'd think "zero cash flow" would not be a viable real estate investment strategy, but in reality it makes sense under the right circumstances. These deals typically have these features:

- They're constructed like a bond.
- That bond must be backed by investment grade rated credit (AAA to BBB) of the tenant.
- A very long-term lease is required (a minimum of 20 years is standard).
- The lease is very closely drawn, and the provisions within that lease essentially make the tenant responsible for all expenses.
- All the rent goes to the institutional lender (thus, the name "zero cash flow").

Generally speaking, Zeroes have one credit tenant and a highly leveraged loan. The loan to value (LTV) will be approximate 88 percent of the property's value.

Zero cash flow deals are not for everyone, but they can work well in situations where a client doesn't need the cash and wants to look to the future in terms of estate planning. He or she will engage in a very high-leveraged transaction to try to amortize the loan for as long as possible. As a result, when the lease is up, their heirs will end up with a property that's free and clear, and those heirs can do what they like with it (vacation of the property and then re-lease of that property for continued income, for example).

Here are some other scenarios where a zero cash flow deal provides the ideal solution in terms of investment and tax deferral.

Situation 1

You've just sold a highly appreciated property and made a considerable amount of money from the deal. However, you don't want to put that money back into this high-priced market. So, you decide to pursue a zero cash flow strategy in the following way:

- You cash out the gain using bond-style refinancing and defer taxes.
- You then reinvest the gain in real estate.
- You'll have completed the trade and be free of the 45-day and 180-day requirements.
- If you make a new investment, it'll have full tax basis, which means you'll end up with a larger portfolio, including the zero cash deal and the new investment.

Situation 2

Perhaps you have a partnership or corporation, and as such you require more depreciable basis to offset current income. Using the zero cash strategy, you can have the most depreciable basis with the least amount of equity out-of-pocket.

Situation 3

Maybe you're concerned that cap rates will increase and potentially reduce or wipe out your equity. Zero cap deals can eliminate this fear because they're "pre-sold" to lenders, who take the risk while you're protected (because cap rates and interest rates fluctuations don't affect the value of zero cash flow deals).

Situation 4

Sometimes investors face foreclosure on their businesses or properties. In these cases, they can make use of zeroes to defer the tax obligation. This is often more desirable than funding deficits on their exiting property, recapitalizing the ownership entity (often called a "hope note"), bankruptcy, or simply handing over the keys to the lender in a taxable event.

In the event of a foreclosure or Deed in Lieu, the investor faces a taxable event with a gain reflecting either the debt forgiven (non-recourse debt) or the fair market value of the property (recourse debt). The amount of gain will also depend on the investor's tax basis in the property. The type of gain (capital or recapture) will depend on the depreciation taken. The tax rates will depend on existing federal and state rates.

102

Situation 5

If security is your primary need, a zero allows you to get that portfolio growing in the safest, most risk-averse possible in the following ways:

- A zero allows you to leverage your tenant's investment grade rating and the "bond" structure to purchase property worth 10 times your equity without personal recourse with;
- debt structures that generally don't balloon for at least 20 years and;
- that are often fully amortized by the tenant's rental payments over the lease term.

Situation 6

Zeroes can be an excellent part of a 1031 Exchange. That's because they can achieve three different objectives for deferring your taxes. Let's assume your objective is to buy debt basis. A zero allows you to buy inexpensive and ready sources of investment grade-rated debt replacement properties for 1031 Exchanges. Purchase a zero for, say, 12 percent equity above the amount of the loan, and the buyer can cover the debt-relief part of the trade with a long-term investment-grade loan and free up equity so you can purchase an additional replacement asset.

If you're in need of passive real estate losses, zeroes can also offset taxable net income with depreciation and interest expense.

Finally, there is the situation where a zero has a "Purchase and Post-Closing Finance" capability. With this option, you can cover both the entire equity and debt from your 1031 trade and subsequently finance out funds. This requires three steps:

- Identify and buy a Zero with all cash (and debt as required).
- The 1031 transaction is completed.
- You can then utilize the option to finance the property up to upwards of 90 percent and distribute or use those financing proceeds. Note that this process allows you to "refinance" with much lower costs. After trading equal

or up for debt replacement purposes, you can access the cash financing proceeds without incurring taxes on the debt boot if cash were disbursed as part of the 1031 transaction.

To complete a 1031 Exchange with a Zero, you'll need to follow these steps:

- Maintain good relationships with lenders and make them aware of your plan.
- Identify a "zero" replacement property.
- Close on the zero replacement property utilizing a Qualified Intermediary (QI). (Note: this step requires you to have equity available for the purchase. The zero will require a smaller amount of equity, which is quite a bit less than alternative investments.)

The benefits of the zero strategy include:

- Owning real estate of the same or greater value.
- Having a credit tenant.
- A portion of the taxes otherwise due deferred and reinvested in real estate.
- Some depreciation, depending on the tax basis.
- A cost study may result in additional depreciation, depending on the property.
- At some point, you may have taxable income from the investment without any cash flow ("phantom income"). The taxable income reflects the unsheltered amount attributable to amortization received as rent.
- You may enjoy asset appreciation, depending on numerous factors.

Summary

As you learned in this chapter, "zero cash flow" transactions are not always easy to understand. That's why we recommend that you always work with brokers who are very experienced in this area.

Now, let's move on to brokers for triple net lease investments. As you'll see in the next chapter, it's extremely important to choose the right one.

About the Real Estate Brokerage Business

Since you'll be dealing with real estate brokerages in terms of triple nets and other investments, it's only fair that you understand the purpose of these firms, and how they work, so you'll be able to evaluate the services they provide.

A brokerage's goal is to bring people together in a profitable manner for all involved. Depending on the type of firm, a broker will connect:

- A seller to a buyer and vice versa
- A landlord to a tenant and vice versa
- An investor to an investment
- A developer to an opportunity

Generally speaking, top brokers tend to fall into two categories – leasing or sales. As you might expect, a leasing broker specializes in leases, and he or she represents a landlord seeking tenants or tenants seeking space.

A sales broker, on the other hand, specializes in representing the buyers and sellers of investment properties. To give you an idea of the respective services provided, let's explore each of these categories.

Leasing Brokers

These brokers can operate in several different areas. For example, they may represent the owner of a building. In this case, an owner signs a Commission Agreement specifying that the broker will find tenants to lease space in the building (or lease the entire building itself). In short, the broker's job is to position the owner's space to lease as quickly as possible and as well as possible.

(Since so many books have been written on residential properties and brokerages, we won't cover that subject in this book. Mortgage brokerages won't be considered either.)

106

Many times, the broker's job involves educating the owner on the market. For example, if an owner is demanding too much (or too little), the broker will need to show that person comparable buildings for lease. This way, the owner can form a basis for lease terms that match the current market.

The broker will often also help with the lease itself in terms of setting the rate and in developing a "concession package." This package consists of incentives for the tenant to lease the space. Such incentives may include free rent for a stated period of time, monies to help the tenant relocate or build out the space, and so forth.

Assuming that during the term of the agreement (usually six months to a year), the broker signs tenants to a lease, and the owner then pays that broker a commission. Many agreements also include a standard provision called a "tail." This provision states that if a lease is signed after the Commission Agreement expires, but if it involves a tenant who saw the building/space during the terms of that agreement, then the broker still earns his or her commission.

As you'd expect, a leasing broker works on commission, and that commission is tied to the total rent a tenant will pay.

Another type of broker is the tenant broker. As the name suggests, these professionals represent companies or individuals in need of leased space. Their job is to locate the space, analyze it and assist in the writing of the lease agreement. In some cases, they're also hired by tenants to negotiate extensions of leases with existing landlords.

Sales (Investment) Brokers

These brokers concentrate on real estate investments and can work for either the seller or the buyer. As with a leasing broker, an investment broker who works for the seller uses a commission agreement that specifies how that broker will be paid upon a sale. The buyer's broker will want an exclusive representation agreement that commits the buyer to work only with that broker for a stated period of time.

Sellers earn their commissions based on the sale price of the property. Generally speaking, the size of the commission depends on the amount of the sale. The larger the sale, the lower the commission (since the total sales amounts are so large).

Customs vary from state to state, but in most cases the seller's broker and the buyer's broker split the commission on a 50/50 basis.

Choosing a Broker

Brokers serve a dual role in that they make sales and uphold a fiduciary responsibility to their clients. Knowing this, you'll want to select one who has a history of maintaining that responsibility with his or her clients.

There are a few brokers out there who focus too much on price and making the sale, instead of serving their clients' best interests. In such cases, the brokers neglect their fiduciary responsibility to maximize the value of their client's assets. Needless to say, that's not good representation. Here's a hypothetical example to illustrate this scenario:

Assume one broker, (Tom) calls up another broker (John) and says, "John, I have a client in a 1031 Exchange looking to buy a Home Depot or similar big box store somewhere in the $10 million range."

John answers, "Well, Tom, I have a Lowe's Center at $12 million, but I'm sure my client will accept $10 million."

In this case, John is not fulfilling his or her responsibility to his client or, in fact, to Tom, the buyer's broker, because he isn't first explaining the value and attributes of the property to Tom and also definitely isn't doing justice to his client who stands to potentially lose $ 2 million.

Unfortunately, the market sometimes attracts people who are more interested in the quick, easy money than their responsibility to clients. This happens because the barriers to entry in the brokerage business are fairly low. It's not hard to become

108

broker. So while there are state testing and ethics guidelines to follow, it's not a Master's thesis-level job.

Knowing this, you should select only experienced, reputable brokers who focus exclusively on triple nets. These professionals will have their fingers on the pulse of market trends. They'll know where the cap rates should be. They'll be able to underwrite the real estate value of a property more easily. They'll have connections within the industry to find and source the deals for different investors. And they'll have more credibility than someone who simply has a real estate license.

To find a broker who understands and meets your triple net lease investment needs, you'll have to do the same thing a brokerage does on a daily basis in the evaluation of properties: conduct due diligence. Investigate various brokers and/or brokerages to make sure they can meet your investment needs. One of the best ways to begin due diligence is to simply sit down and write out your objectives in terms of triple-net leases. This will focus your thinking, and, at the same time, it'll provide the broker with a set of broad guidelines to work with.

Investigate different brokers via the Internet, via their literature (brochures, promotional literature, and so forth), and through direct contact. This will give you a sense of their respective histories and their success in the market. Check out "word of mouth" among your friends and associates as well as any references available.

When you're doing your homework, look closely at the length of time that the broker has been in business. Generally speaking, the longer the better. You definitely don't want to work with beginners in this highly complex business. There's just too much money at stake.

Other key considerations include the broker's credentials, certification and education in the field of commercial real estate. Ask yourself questions like: Do they have the correct credentials? Are they highly educated in their field? Do they keep up with the changes in the market and their particular field?

When you make direct contact with a brokerage, get to know the staff members. This will give you an idea of their level of professionalism and effectiveness in handling people and transactions. A good brokerage will have highly-educated staff members who are adept at meeting your needs in an efficient manner. Of course, this action will also give you a good sense of whether or not your personalities will mesh.

Summary

In terms of triple net lease investments, look to establish and maintain a long relationship of trust with a solid, respected, and experienced broker. He or she should be able to bring people together and get a deal done that's profitable for all involved.

Remember, there's a lot of money involved with triple net leases. You definitely want to work with someone who's savvy and sophisticated in these types of properties.

Ready, Set, Go!

We sincerely hope you've enjoyed our book on triple net leases. It's based on the decades of experience and knowledge that we've racked up in this specialized industry, and we're happy to share it with you in hopes that it makes your investment journey smoother, easier and more profitable.

As we mentioned early this book, triple net leases don't sound too exciting until you realize just how beneficial they can be to your financial situation.

Here's a quick overview of those benefits:

- Lower-risk income
- Preservation of capital
- Tax deferral
- Relief from management obligations
- Provision of estate assets for your heirs.

If we've whetted your appetite for triple net lease investment opportunities, we suggest you dig deeper into the subject to determine if these options are appropriate for your particular needs and desires. If they are, be sure to put the necessary time and effort into assembling a reliable investment team and conducting due diligence before signing on the dotted line.

Don't forget to contact a reputable broker and ask him or her about the information and questions outlined in the chapter "About the Real Estate Brokerage Business." This will help ensure your chances of success and give you invaluable insights that would take years or even decades to learn on your own.

Armed with the knowledge you're taking away from this book and a good broker, we know you'll enjoy a profitable journey. Good luck!

Appendix A

Sample Triple Net Lease Agreement

LEASE_____

By this Lease, made the _____ day of _____, 2010, between DAVIS LIMITED PARTNERSHIP, an Illinois limited partnership, hereinafter called "Landlord", and THE DRUG STORE., an Illinois corporation, hereinafter called "Tenant";

1. Landlord hereby leases to Tenant, and Tenant hereby rents from Landlord, for an Initial Term (as defined in Article 3(a) herein) and a Term of sixty (60) years commencing on July 1, 2010, and continuing to and including June 30, 2070 (as such dates shall be adjusted pursuant to Article 3(b) herein and subject to prior termination as hereinafter provided), the premises to include both the real property and existing building and other improvements located at the southwest corner of Kirkwood Road and Lee Highway, in the City of Arlington, County of Arlington, Commonwealth of Virginia, together with all improvements, appurtenances, easements, and privileges belonging thereto. The existing building includes approximately 80 feet of frontage along Lee Highway and approximately 141 feet of depth, being an area containing 10,971 square feet of first floor area and 726 square feet on a mezzanine level for a total of 11,697 square feet (the "Building"). All of the foregoing is shown on the site plan attached hereto and made a part hereof as Exhibit "A" (the "Site Plan"), and as legally described in Exhibit "B" attached hereto and made a part hereof. The Building, real estate, and other improvements are hereinafter collectively referred to as the "Leased Premises."

(Remainder of page intentionally left blank.)

THE TERMS, COVENANTS AND CONDITIONS OF SAID LETTING ARE AS FOLLOWS:

RENT

2. Tenant shall pay rent for the Leased Premises as follows:

(a) (i) A fixed rent of $41,666.66 per month, commencing on the Rent Commencement Date (as defined in Article 6), and continuing to and including the last day of the one hundred twentieth (120th) full calendar month of the Term;

(ii) A fixed rent of $45,833.33 per month, commencing on the first day of the one hundred twenty first (121st) full calendar month of the Term and continuing to and including the last day of the two hundred fortieth (240th) full calendar month of the Term;

(iii) A fixed rent of $50,416.66 per month, commencing on the first day of the two hundred forty first (241st) full calendar month of the Term and continuing to and including the last day of the three hundred sixtieth (360th) full calendar month of the Term;

114

(iv) A fixed rent of $55,458.33 per month, commencing on the first day of the three hundred sixty first (361st) full calendar month of the Term and continuing to and including the last day of the four hundred eightieth (480th) full calendar month of the Term;

(v) A fixed rent of $61,004.16 per month, commencing on the first day of the four hundred eighty first (481st) full calendar month of the Term and continuing to and including the last day of the six hundredth (600th) full calendar month of the Term; and

(vi) A fixed rent of $67,104.58 per month, commencing on the first day of the six hundred first (601st) full calendar month of the Term and continuing thereafter for the remainder of the Term of this Lease. Fixed rent shall be payable on the first day of each and every month in advance (without demand, deduction or set off except as specifically set forth herein) and shall be properly apportioned for any period less than a full calendar month.

(b) Until further notice by Landlord to Tenant, rent checks shall be payable to and mailed to:

Davis Limited Partnership   100 Main Street Suite 20, Barrington, Illinois 60010   Phone: 000-000-0000 Fax: 000-000-0000

Landlord's FEIN: _____

1099 Recipient:

Davis Limited Partnership   100 Main Street Suite 20, Barrington, Illinois 60010

Phone: 000-000-0000 Fax: 000-000-0000

(c) Landlord shall, prior to the first day of the Term, provide Tenant (Attn.: Corporate and Transactional Law Department, Real Estate Group, PO Box 100, Chicago, IL 00000) with a completed IRS Form W-9. Any successor to Landlord shall likewise provide Tenant with such completed IRS Form W-9 as a condition precedent to any rent or other payment from Tenant.

INITIAL TERM, TERM, RENT COMMENCEMENT, LEASE YEAR, OPTIONS

3. (a) Initial Term. The Initial Term shall commence on the date that the Landlord delivers possession of the of the Leased Premises in accordance with Article 4 of this Lease (the "Possession Date"), and continuing to and including the day immediately preceding the day that the Term of this Lease commences as provided hereinafter in paragraph (b) of this Article 3 (the "Initial Term").

(b) Term. The Term shall be adjusted so that it commences on the Rent Commencement Date (as defined in Article 6), and shall continue for sixty (60) years thereafter (the "Term"); provided, however, that if such Rent Commencement Date be other than the first day of the calendar month, then the Term shall continue to and include the last day of the same calendar month of the sixtieth (60th) year thereafter.

(c) Lease Year. The first lease year shall commence on the Rent Commencement Date and, if such date shall be on the first day of a calendar month, shall end twelve months thereafter, or, if such date be other than the first day of a calendar month, shall end on the last day of the same calendar month of the first year thereafter, and each succeeding lease year shall be each succeeding twelve month period.

(d) Termination Options. Tenant shall have the right and option, at Tenant's election, to terminate this Lease effective as of the last day of the two hundred fortieth (240th) full calendar month of the Term, effective as of the last day of the three hundredth (300th) full calendar month of the Term, effective as of the last day of the three hundred sixtieth (360th) full calendar month of the Term, effective as of the last day of the four hundred twentieth (420th) full calendar month of the Term, effective as of the last day of the four hundred eightieth (480th) full calendar month of the Term, effective as of the last day of the five hundred fortieth (540th) full calendar month of the Term, effective as of the last day of the six hundredth (600th) full calendar month of the Term, and effective as of the last day of the six hundredth sixtieth (660th) full calendar month of the Term. If Tenant shall elect to exercise any such option, Tenant shall send notice thereof to Landlord, at least nine (9) months prior to the date this Lease shall so terminate, but no notice shall be required to terminate this Lease upon the expiration of the Term.

DELIVERY OF POSSESSION

4. (a) Landlord shall put Tenant into exclusive physical possession of the Leased Premises on or before April 1, 2010, or as soon as possible thereafter, and in any case not later than June 15, 2010. Landlord shall send written notice to Tenant's Divisional Vice President of Construction, Corporate and Transactional Law Department, Real Estate Group, PO Box 100, Chicago, IL 00000 with copy to Tenant's Corporate and Transactional Law Department, Real Estate Group, at least seven (7) days (but not more than thirty (30) days) before such possession is to be delivered. As a condition precedent to the delivery of possession of the Leased Premises to Tenant, the obligations of the Landlord described in Articles 18 of this Lease shall have been completed and satisfied. Landlord shall deliver exclusive physical possession of the Leased Premises to Tenant on the date set forth in Landlord's notice. If possession has not been delivered to Tenant on or prior to June 15, 2010 because either (w) Landlord has not been able to obtain the "Zoning Evidence" (hereinafter described and defined in Article 18) due to any act or condition that is beyond the reasonable control of the Landlord, or (x) Landlord has notified the Tenant of Landlord's good faith determination that continued efforts to obtain Zoning Evidence would be futile, then Landlord shall send written notice of the foregoing failure to the Tenant on or before May 31, 2010 (the "Failure to Deliver Notice"). Upon receipt of the Failure to Deliver Notice, Tenant shall be entitled, as its exclusive remedy and in its sole and absolute discretion, by written notice of election sent to the Landlord within seven (7) days after receipt of the Failure to Deliver Notice to either (y) terminate this Lease, upon which termination Landlord shall immediately refund any and all amounts previously paid by Tenant to Landlord and neither party shall have any further rights or obligations hereunder, or (z) accept delivery of possession and waive the Zoning Evidence obligation under Article 18 hereof. If possession is not delivered by July 1, 2010 for any reason, Tenant, in addition to Tenant's remedies under this Lease, may cancel this Lease by notice to Landlord. In no event shall Tenant be entitled to any consequential damages in exercising any right granted in this Article 4(a). Except as set forth in Article 18 and except as otherwise expressly provided for in

116

this Lease, Tenant agrees to accept the Leased Premises at delivery of possession in "as is", "where is" condition.

(b) Subject to all rights of the current tenant of the Premises, the Landlord has heretofore allowed and with reasonable prior notice during the period ending on March 31, 2010 (the 'Inspection Period") will continue to allow the Tenant and its representatives the right to enter upon the Leased Premises to take measurements and otherwise perform such non-invasive investigations and to obtain or perform such studies and reports as Tenant deems necessary or appropriate including, but not limited to: the presence of any hazardous substances located in, on or under the Leased Premises; the existing condition of all building systems in the Leased Premises and the Building; the existing condition of the parking areas of the Leased Premises; and the existing condition of other elements of the Leased Premises and the Building. Such entry shall not constitute a waiver as to any other obligations of Landlord hereunder.

(c) During the Inspection Period Tenant shall use good faith efforts to obtain from appropriate governmental authorities having jurisdiction thereof building permits, site plan approvals, plan of development approvals, special exceptions, special or conditional use permits, variances, licenses and other permits required (i) to permit Tenant to perform Tenant's Construction, as defined in Article 5, (ii) to install all signage desired by Tenant for its business (including but not limited to a monument identification sign in such location and dimension as is acceptable to Tenant), (iii) to operate the existing drive through facility in connection with Tenant's business, (iv) to install and operate a satellite dish on the Leased Premises, and (v) to conduct its business on the Leased Premises (including without limitation all licenses, permits and approvals so as to enable Tenant to operate a prescription pharmacy at the Leased Premises). The foregoing shall hereinafter be referred to, collectively and inclusively as "Tenant's Approvals."

(d) If the Tenant shall not be satisfied with respect to the results of the investigations made by Tenant pursuant to paragraph (b) of this Article or the results of its efforts to obtain Tenant Approvals pursuant to paragraph (c) of this Article, Tenant may terminate this Lease by written notice delivered to Landlord not later than the expiration of the Inspection Period, time being of the essence. In the event Tenant fails to terminate this Lease, Tenant shall be deemed to have waived its right to terminate the Lease pursuant to this Article 4(d). Tenant shall have no obligation to accept delivery of possession of the Leased Premises under Article 4(a) until Landlord has complied with the provisions of Article 18.

TENANT'S CONSTRUCTION

5. (a) In order to adapt and equip the Leased Premises for Tenant's use and occupancy, certain additions, removals, alterations, improvements, installations and construction of a non-structural nature, all hereinafter called "Tenant's Construction," will be required. All of Tenant's Construction shall be done by Tenant, at Tenant's sole cost and expense, in accordance with Tenant's plans and specifications, and shall be done in a good and workmanlike manner, free and clear of liens for labor and materials furnished Tenant.

(b) Landlord and Tenant acknowledge that pursuant to the Arlington County, Virginia Zoning Ordinance the existing drive-through facility attached to the Building does not conform to current zoning provisions; accordingly, the continued use by Tenant of the drive-through facility will prohibit the Tenant from (i) making structural alterations to the Building except those required by law or ordinance, and/or (ii) adding to or enlarging the Building in any manner unless in each of the foregoing instances, the Tenant first obtains a special use permit from the Arlington County Board to operate a drive through facility. If Tenant intends to make any structural changes to the Building notwithstanding the foregoing described consequences, such Tenant's Construction of a structural nature shall not be performed without first obtaining Landlord's written consent, which consent shall not be unreasonably withheld. Landlord has furnished to Tenant architectural drawings relating to the Building located on the Leased Premises and such other plans as Landlord may presently have in its possession relative to the Leased Premises so that Tenant may be enabled to prepare and furnish to Landlord those portions of Tenant's plans and specifications calling for structural changes to the Leased Premises ("Structural Plans"). Landlord agrees to approve or reject Tenant's Structural Plans within seven (7) days after receipt from Tenant, and if not approved or rejected within said period, Tenant's Structural Plans shall be deemed approved. In the event Landlord shall reject Tenant's Structural Plans within the period above provided, then Landlord shall return Tenant's Structural Plans to Tenant indicating the items so rejected. Tenant shall then have fifteen (15) days to resubmit Tenant's Structural Plans to Landlord, and Landlord shall have seven (7) days for approval or rejection, and if not approved or rejected within said period, Tenant's Structural Plans shall be deemed approved. Landlord shall not withhold its approval of Tenant's Structural Plans provided they (1) are in compliance with national, state and local code requirements, and (2) meet acceptable standards of architectural and engineering practice.

(d) Upon the written request of Tenant and at no out of pocket third party cost or expense to Landlord, Landlord agrees to execute or join in the execution of any documents or instruments that may be reasonably required by Tenant and/or third parties, including but not limited to governmental authorities for the development, use and enjoyment of the Leased Premises. Without limitation, such documentation may (i) include zoning applications, (ii) changes or variances required by governmental authority, (iii) dedications of easements for utilities and other purposes as Tenant may reasonably require (iv) building permits, variances, use permits, licenses, approvals or similar governmental authorizations, and (v) other like matters.

RENT COMMENCEMENT

6. Tenant shall commence paying fixed rents pursuant to Article 2 hereof as of the date that is the earlier to occur of: (a) July 10, 2010; or (b) the date Tenant's store opens for business to the general public (the "Rent Commencement Date"). Anything to the contrary in this Lease notwithstanding, Tenant shall have no obligation to pay rent or other charges until Landlord has provided all of the information and instruments required by Article 18 of this Lease. Nothing contained in this Lease shall be construed to obligate Tenant (or its successors or assigns) to open its store for business to the general public or to continue to operate its store in the Leased Premises.

PARKING

7. Tenant, at Tenant's cost and expense, shall maintain, repair and replace the parking areas of the Leased Premises. However, Tenant shall have no obligation to perform or pay any costs in connection with any damages caused by the acts or omissions of Landlord. The foregoing shall remain Landlord's responsibility to perform. The parking areas of the Leased Premises shall be for the exclusive use of Tenant and Tenant's customers, employees, invitees, successors, assigns and sub lessees.

EXCLUSIVES

8. (a) Landlord covenants and agrees that, during the Term and any extensions or renewals thereof, no additional property which Landlord, directly or indirectly, may now or hereafter

own, lease or control, and which is contiguous to, or which is within five hundred (500) feet of any boundary of, the Leased Premises (the "Landlord's Property"), will be used for any one or combination of the following: (i) the operation of a drug store or a so-called prescription pharmacy or prescription ordering, processing or delivery facility, whether or not a pharmacist is present at such facility, or for any other purpose requiring a qualified pharmacist or other person authorized by law to dispense medicinal drugs, directly or indirectly, for a fee or remuneration of any kind; (ii) the operation of a medical diagnostic lab or the provision of treatment services (other than as part of a medical, dental, physician, surgical or chiropractic office[s], which office[s] shall not be restricted by this subclause [ii]); (iii) the sale of so-called health and beauty aids or drug sundries; (iv) the operation of a business in which photofinishing services (including, without limitation, digital photographic processing or printing, or the sale of any other imaging services, processes or goods) or photographic film are offered for sale; (v) the operation of a business in which greeting cards or gift wrap are offered for sale; and (vi) the operation of a business in which prepackaged food items for off premises consumption are offered for sale. In the event that Tenant files suit against any party to enforce the foregoing restrictions, Landlord agrees to cooperate fully with Tenant in the prosecution of any such suit, and reimburse Tenant for all of the reasonable attorneys' fees and court costs incurred by Tenant in connection with such suit, provided that Tenant prevails in such litigation. For purposes hereof "contiguous" shall mean property that is either adjoining the Leased Premises or separated from the Leased Premises only by a public or private street, alley or right-of-way.

(b) In addition, Landlord shall not permit or suffer any other occupant of Landlord's Property to use any premises or any portion thereof for purposes of a cocktail lounge, bar, any other establishment that sells alcoholic beverages for on-premises consumption (other than in conjunction with a full service table restaurant), disco, bowling alley, pool hall, billiard parlor, skating rink, roller rink, amusement arcade, a theater of any kind, children's play or party facility, adult bookstore, adult theatre, adult amusement facility, any facility selling or displaying pornographic materials or having such displays, second hand store, odd lot, closeout or liquidation store, auction house, flea market, educational or training facility (including, without limitation, a beauty school, barber college, school or other facility catering primarily to students or trainees rather than customers), gymnasium, sport or health club or spa, blood bank, massage parlor, funeral home, sleeping quarters or lodging, the outdoor housing or raising of animals, the sale, leasing or storage of automobiles, boats or other vehicles, any industrial use (including, without limitation, any manufacturing, smelting, rendering, brewing, refining, chemical manufacturing or processing, or other manufacturing uses), any mining or mineral exploration or development except by non-surface means, a car wash, a carnival, amusement park or circus, an assembly hall, off track betting establishment, bingo hall, any use involving the use, storage, disposal or handling of hazardous materials or underground storage tanks, any use which may materially or adversely affect the water and sewer services supplied to the Leased Premises, a church, temple, synagogue, mosque, or other house of worship, any facility for the sale of paraphernalia for use with illicit drugs, office use (except incidental to a retail use and as permitted by Article 8(a)(ii) above), or any use which creates a nuisance.

(c) In the event that any action, claim or suit is brought by any party against Tenant alleging that Tenant's operations on the Leased Premises are in violation of any use restriction contained in any instrument, Landlord shall defend (by counsel reasonably satisfactory to Tenant), indemnify and hold Tenant harmless from any damages, loss, or cost (including, without limitation, attorneys' fees and costs) suffered by Tenant thereby, or from the enforcement of said restriction against Tenant. No encumbrance, lien, or restriction recorded against or otherwise imposed upon the Leased Premises shall be binding upon or otherwise enforceable against Tenant or its successors and assigns unless Tenant has expressly and in writing, consented to said recordation or imposition; any such purported encumbrance, lien or restriction to which Tenant has not consented shall be void. The foregoing restriction against the imposition or recordation of other liens, encumbrances or restrictions shall be deemed a covenant running with the land in addition to any contractual obligation of Landlord.

UTILITIES

9. Tenant shall pay when due all bills for water, sewer rents, sewer charges, heat, gas, phone and electricity used in the Building or on the Leased Premises from and after the Possession Date until the expiration of the Term. All utilities should be in Landlord's name prior to the Possession Date. Tenant shall place the utilities in its name from and after the Possession Date. Landlord shall be responsible for all utility bills for the period prior to the Possession Date. In the event the utility company requires that a prior bill be paid in order to establish service in Tenant's name, Tenant may pay such bill and Landlord shall reimburse Tenant the amount paid upon receipt of an invoice. If Landlord fails to so reimburse Tenant, Tenant may deduct the amount due from all sums due Landlord under this Lease.

REPAIRS, CONFORMITY WITH THE LAW

10. (a) (i) Tenant, at Tenant's sole cost and expense, shall maintain the Leased Premises and make all necessary repairs and replacements, whether interior or exterior, to all parts of the same. Upon delivery of possession of the Leased Premises to Tenant, Landlord shall cause all contractor's and manufacturer's warranties and guaranties, if any, relating to the Leased Premises to be assigned to Tenant, or to the extent not assignable, then to be issued in Tenant's name.

(ii) Prior to the date of execution of this Lease, Tenant, at Tenant's sole cost and expense, has caused a non-invasive study and report in accordance with American Society For Testing and Materials Standard Practice for Environmental Site Assessment Process, current edition, to be performed by a state certified environmental engineer or contractor, determining the presence of any Hazardous Substances including, but not limited to, the existence of any underground storage tanks, and/or petroleum or petroleum by-products located in, on or under the Leased Premises (the "Environmental Report"). Such report shall be certified in writing to Tenant and a copy shall be delivered to Landlord prior to the expiration of the Inspection Period. Except as set forth in Article 18 and except as otherwise expressly provided for in this Lease, in the event Tenant does not terminate this Lease during the Inspection Period, Tenant agrees to accept the Leased Premises at delivery of possession in "as is," "where is" condition. Landlord and Tenant acknowledge and agree that Tenant shall be entitled to terminate this Lease prior to the expiration of the Inspection Period in the event the Environmental Report discloses the need for removal or remediation of any Hazardous Substances.

(iii) If, after commencement of the Term, any Hazardous Substance is discovered at any time in, under or about the Leased Premises or any part(s) thereof (unless introduced by Tenant) which is required to be removed or remediate by Environmental Law and which interferes with Tenant's ability to operate at the Leased Premises, Landlord, at Landlord's expense, shall remove and dispose of the same in the manner described in and provide all reasonable documentation as Tenant may require. If Landlord's work or removal under this Article 10(a)(iii) shall interfere with or disrupt the use or operations at the Leased Premises, then without limitation of Tenant's rights or remedies as a result thereof, the rent and other sums due by Tenant shall abate until the interference or disruption shall cease. Any remedial action plans required for Landlord's work or remediation under this Article 10(a)(iii) shall be subject to the prior express written consent of Tenant. Tenant's consent may be conditioned upon, among other things, determining that the required remediation plans will not interfere with

120

Tenant's use or occupancy of the Leased Premises and that no liability or obligations shall be imposed upon or incurred by Tenant in connection therewith. Landlord hereby indemnifies, saves and holds Tenant harmless and shall defend Tenant from and against any claims, liability, obligation, damage, cost, expense, fines and penalties, including, without limitation, attorneys' fees and costs, resulting directly or indirectly from the presence, removal or disposal of any such Hazardous Substance not introduced by Tenant. In the event that any Hazardous Substance is discovered at any time in, under or about the Leased Premises which has been introduced by Tenant, Tenant shall, at Tenant's expense, remove and dispose of the same. Tenant hereby indemnifies, saves and holds Landlord harmless and shall defend Landlord from and against any claims, liability, obligation, damage, cost, expense, fines and penalties, including, without limitation, attorneys' fees and costs, resulting directly or indirectly from the presence, removal or disposal of any such Hazardous Substance introduced into the Leased Premises solely by Tenant. The foregoing indemnifications shall survive the termination or expiration of this Lease for any reason.

(iv) "Hazardous Substance" shall mean any hazardous or toxic chemical, waste, byproduct, pollutant, contaminant, compound, product or substance, including, without limitation, asbestos, polychlorinated biphenyl's, petroleum (including crude oil or any fraction or byproduct thereof), and any material the exposure to, or manufacture, possession, presence, use, generation, storage, transportation, treatment, release, disposal, abatement, cleanup, removal, remediation or handling of which is prohibited, controlled or regulated by any Environmental Law.

(v) "Environmental Law" shall mean any federal, state, regional, county or local governmental statute, law, regulation, ordinance, order or code or any consent decree, judgment, permit, license, code, covenant, deed restriction, common law, or other requirement, presently in effect or hereafter created, issued and/or adopted, pertaining to protection of the environment, health or safety of persons, natural resources, conservation, wildlife, waste management, and pollution (including, without limitation, regulation of releases and disposals to air, land, water and ground water), including, without limitation, the Comprehensive Environmental Response, Compensation and Liability Act of 1980, as amended by the Superfund Amendments and Reauthorization Act of 1986, 42 U.S.C. 9601 et seq., Solid Waste Disposal Act, as amended by the Resource Conservation and Recovery Act of 1976 and Solid and Hazardous Waste Amendments of 1984, 42 U.S.C. 6901 et seq., Federal Water Pollution Control Act, as amended by the Clean Water Act of 1977, 33 U.S.C. 1251 et seq., Clean Air Act of 1966, as amended, 42 U.S.C. 7401 et seq., Toxic Substances Control Act of 1976, 15 U.S.C. 2601 et seq., Occupational Safety and Health Act of 1970, as amended, 29 U.S.C. 651 et seq., Emergency Planning and Community Right-to-Know Act of 1986, 42 U.S.C. 11001 et seq., National Environmental Policy Act of 1975, 42 U.S.C. 300(f) et seq., and all amendments as well as any similar state or local statute or code and replacements of any of the same and rules, regulations, guidance documents and publications promulgated thereunder.

(c) Subject to Landlord's obligations under Article 5(d), Tenant shall make all changes and installations, and pay the cost, if any, of all inspections must comply with the valid requirements of public authorities as they apply to the Leased Premises or the Building.

SIGNS, TENANT'S FIXTURES

11. (a) Tenant may install and operate interior and exterior electric and other signs. Tenant shall have the right to install mechanical equipment, including satellite dishes or other antennae for telecommunications affixed to the roof or other portions of the Building or other portions of the Leased Premises. Tenant may also install pay telephones, automatic teller machines and

other electronic consumer service apparatus on the Leased Premises. With respect to each of the foregoing installations, Tenant shall comply with all lawful requirements.

(b) Tenant shall at all times have the right to remove all fixtures, machinery, equipment, appurtenances and other property furnished or installed by Tenant or by Landlord at Tenant's expense, it being expressly understood and agreed that said property shall not become part of the Building or Leased Premises but shall at all times be and remain the personal property of Tenant and shall not be subject to any Landlord's lien. Notwithstanding anything to the contrary herein, in no event shall Tenant be required to remove the electric conveyor from the Leased Premises at the expiration or earlier termination of this Lease.

ALTERATIONS

12. (a) At any time and from time to time, Tenant, at Tenant's cost and expense, and in compliance with applicable law (and subject to Section 5(b)), may make such structural and non-structural alterations and additions to the Leased Premises as Tenant desires, provided that any such alteration or addition when completed shall be of such character as not to diminish the structural integrity, leasable square footage or fair market value of the Building. Title to any alterations or additions made by Tenant shall vest in Landlord, and Tenant shall deliver such documents of conveyance thereof as Landlord may reasonably request at the expiration or sooner termination of this Lease. Landlord shall cooperate at no out of pocket cost to Landlord in securing necessary permits and approvals. Tenant shall not permit any mechanics' or other liens to stand against the Leased Premises for work or material furnished Tenant.

(b) Landlord covenants and agrees that Landlord shall not make any alterations or additions to the Leased Premises without Tenant's written consent. Landlord shall not permit any mechanics' or other liens to stand against the Leased Premises for work or material furnished to Landlord.

ASSIGNMENT AND SUBLETTING

13. (a) At any time and from time to time, Tenant may discontinue the operation of its business (if any) in the Leased Premises or Building.

(b) At any time and from time to time, Tenant's interest under this Lease may, be assigned and re-assigned, without Landlord's consent, provided that any such assignment or reassignment be only to a corporation or other entity which is subsidiary to or affiliated with Tenant, or to a corporation or other entity resulting from any consolidation, reorganization or merger to which Tenant, or any of its parent, subsidiaries or affiliates, may be a party. At any time and from time to time, without Landlord's consent, Tenant may also sublet or license or permit a portion or portions of the Building or Leased Premises to be used for concessions, leased or licensed departments and demonstrations in connection with and as part of the operation of Tenant's business.

(c) At any time and from time to time, without Landlord's consent, Tenant may sublet a portion of the Leased Premises, to any person, firm, corporation or other entity, other than a corporation or other entity described in Article 13(b) above, for any lawful purpose. At any time and from time to time, without Landlord's consent, Tenant may assign this Lease or Tenant may sublet the Leased Premises or Building to any person, firm, corporation or other entity, other than a corporation or other entity described in Article 13(b) above, for any lawful purpose.

(d) In the event of a subletting of all or a portion of the Leased Premises or Building, and upon Tenant's request, Landlord shall promptly furnish and deliver to Tenant, in form and substance reasonably acceptable to Tenant, an agreement executed by Landlord, obligating Landlord to be bound as Landlord by any such sublease and by all of the subtenant's rights thereunder in the event that this Lease is terminated for any reason; provided, however, that (i) Landlord's obligations under such sublease shall be no greater than Landlord's obligations under this Lease; (ii) that the subtenant's obligations under such sublease shall be no less than Tenant's obligations under this Lease and, (iii) the subtenant has cured any breach of this Lease.

(e) Notwithstanding any assignment of this Lease, Walgreen Co. shall not be released from liability, except that Walgreen Co. shall be released only to the extent the Lease is modified or amended in any respect so as to increase Tenant's liability thereunder without the prior written approval of Walgreen Co. In the event of a default by any such assignee, Landlord shall give Walgreen Co. notice of such default, shall accept cure of such default by Walgreen Co. within thirty (30) days after such notice and shall permit Walgreen Co. to re-enter and repossess the Leased Premises for the then unelapsed portion of the Term of this Lease upon all of the provisions of this Lease.

CASUALTY

14. (a) If all or any portion of the Building or any improvements in, on or under the Leased Premises shall be damaged or destroyed by fire or other casualty required to be insured (or self-insured) by Tenant pursuant to Article 20, then Tenant shall repair and restore the Building and said improvements to (i) their condition immediately prior to such damage or destruction or (ii) a condition similar in nature to those buildings then being constructed by or on behalf of Tenant at the time of the damage or destruction, without abatement of rent. Except for the obligations and liabilities of Tenant set forth in this Article 14, Tenant shall have no other obligations or liabilities with respect to such casualty.

(b) Notwithstanding the foregoing, in the event the Building is damaged or destroyed by fire or other casualty to the extent of fifteen percent (15 percent) or more thereof and such casualty occurs after the first day of the two hundred sixteenth (216th) full calendar month of the Term, Tenant may cancel this Lease by notice to Landlord. If Tenant has so canceled this Lease and the fire or other casualty is an insurable casualty under Tenant's special form coverage insurance, Tenant shall provide Landlord with the proceeds of such insurance in an amount required by Article 20 of this Lease plus the amount of any deductible. If Tenant self-insures, then Tenant shall pay the amount required in the previous sentence as if Tenant had obtained insurance from a third party. Any proceeds payable by Tenant to Landlord under this Article 14(b) shall be exclusive of the cost of improvements made by or on behalf of Tenant to the Leased Premises or Building.

LANDLORD'S RIGHT TO INSPECT

15. Landlord may at reasonable times during Tenant's business hours, and after so advising Tenant, enter the Building for the purpose of examining the condition of the Leased Premises, but not so as to interfere with Tenant's business.

SURRENDER

16. At the expiration or termination of this Lease, Tenant shall surrender immediate possession of the Leased Premises in good condition, broom clean subject to reasonable wear and tear,

changes and alterations, and damage by fire, casualty and the elements. Any holding over by Tenant shall not operate, except by written agreement, to extend or renew this Lease or to imply or create a new lease, but in case of any such holdover, Landlord's remedies shall be limited to either the immediate termination of Tenant's occupancy or the treatment of Tenant's occupancy as a month to month tenancy, any custom or law allowing other remedies or damages or which may be to the contrary notwithstanding. In the event Tenant shall holdover possession of the Leased Premises, Tenant shall be liable to Landlord for Rent and/or damages equal to, in the case of each month of holdover 125 percent of the Rent for such Premises in effect during the such Premises in effect during the last month of the Term, plus in all cases 100 percent of Real Estate Taxes and all other amount required under this Lease for the Leased Premises and other amounts due hereunder.

DEFAULT AND REMEDIES

17. (a) If any fixed rent is due and remains unpaid for ten (10) days after receipt of notice from Landlord, or if Tenant breaches any of the other promises and covenants of this Lease and if such other breach continues for thirty (30) days after receipt of notice from Landlord, Landlord shall then but not until then, have the right to sue for rent and other charges due from time to time under the terms of this Lease, or the right to re-enter the Leased Premises with or without termination as hereinafter provided in this Article 17; but if Tenant shall pay said fixed rent within said ten (10) days, or in good faith within said thirty (30) days commence to correct such other breach, and diligently proceed therewith to completion, then Tenant shall not be considered in default. Notwithstanding the foregoing, should Tenant be in default, after notice and expiration of the applicable cure period provided above in this Article 17(a), Landlord shall not be entitled to terminate this Lease and re-enter the Leased Premises as a result thereof if Tenant's default shall not be deemed material, or if Tenant's failure to perform is the result of a good faith dispute as to Tenant's obligation(s) under the terms of this Lease. In the event that Tenant shall be considered in default, after notice and an opportunity to cure as herein provided, in any obligation of Tenant under this Lease which under then applicable Virginia law would permit Landlord to terminate this Lease, then and in such event Landlord may either terminate this Lease or instead Landlord may elect, without terminating this Lease, to re-enter the Leased Premises by process of law and relet the same for such term and such rentals as Landlord shall in the exercise of its best efforts be able to obtain at the time of such reletting. Upon such reletting by Landlord, the rents and all other sums received by Landlord from such reletting shall be applied first, to the payment of the reasonable costs and expenses of such reletting (including reasonable brokers commissions that Landlord may incur in connection with such reletting pertaining to or calculated on only the period between the commencement of the lease term of the replacement tenant and prior to the last day of the 240th full calendar month of the Term); second, to the payment of rent and other charges due hereunder from Tenant to Landlord; and the residue, if any, shall be held by Landlord and applied in the payment of future rent and other charges as the same may become due and payable hereunder. Tenant shall have no obligation to pay any of Landlord's alteration or renovation costs. If the rents and other sums received from such reletting during any month are less than the rents and other sums to be paid during that month by Tenant hereunder, Tenant shall pay any such deficiency to Landlord. Such deficiency shall be calculated and paid monthly. If Landlord elects to repossess the Leased Premises without terminating this Lease, as herein provided, Landlord shall use its best efforts to relet the Leased Premises as above stated and shall be obligated to take all steps necessary to mitigate its damages. In the event Landlord re-enters the Leased Premises without terminating the Lease as herein provided, then this Lease shall be deemed terminated at the next available termination date set forth in Article 3(d); at which time Tenant shall be released of all further unaccrued liability under this Lease. Nothing contained herein shall prohibit tenant from exercising any option or right to which it may be entitled under this Lease or at law or equity to terminate this Lease, and upon the exercise of such

option or right of termination Tenant shall be released of all further unaccrued liability under this Lease. Nothing contained herein shall permit Landlord to accelerate any rental or other sums due by Tenant under this Lease. The foregoing remedies of Landlord shall be exclusive and are in lieu of any other remedies to which Landlord may now or hereafter be entitled to at law; provided however that Landlord shall, in the event of a default by Tenant, after notice and opportunity to cure as herein set forth, be entitled to pursue any equitable remedies to which Landlord may be entitled.

The occurrence of three (3) consecutive defaults by Tenant in the payment of fixed rent shall be deemed a material default. As part of any cure of Tenant's failure to pay fixed rent or other amounts hereunder when due, Landlord shall be entitled to collect interest on such past due amounts (commencing from the due date) at the so-called prime rate charged from time to time by Bank of America (its successors and assigns), plus two percent (2 percent) until fully reimbursed.

(b) If Landlord shall from time to time fail to perform any act or acts required of Landlord by this Lease and if such failure continues for thirty (30) days after receipt of notice from Tenant, Tenant shall then have the right, in addition to such remedies as may be available under law or in equity, at Tenant's option, to perform such act or acts, in such manner as Tenant deems reasonably necessary, and the full amount of the cost and expense so incurred shall immediately be owing by Landlord to Tenant, and Tenant shall have the right and is hereby irrevocably authorized and directed to deduct such amount from fixed rent and other sums due Landlord, together with interest thereon at the so-called prime rate charged from time to time by Bank of America (its successors and assigns), plus two percent (2 percent) until fully reimbursed. If Landlord shall in good faith within said thirty (30) days commence to correct such breach, and diligently proceed therewith to completion, then Landlord shall not be considered in default.

(c) No delay on the part of either party in enforcing any of the provisions of this Lease shall be considered as a waiver thereof. Any consent or approval granted by either party under this Lease must be in writing and shall not be deemed to waive or render unnecessary the obtaining of consent or approval with respect to any subsequent act or omission for which consent is required or sought.

TITLE AND POSSESSION

18. (a) (i) Landlord covenants, represents and warrants to Tenant as follows: (1) that Landlord has entered into a contract to acquire fee simple title to the Leased Premises; (2) that Landlord has the full right, power and authority, without the consent or approval of any other party (except the consent of the existing tenant to terminate its existing lease, which has been obtained by Landlord), to enter into this Lease and perform the obligations on the part of the Landlord to be kept and performed; (3) that said entire property comprising the Leased Premises is now and shall be as of the date of the recording of a Memorandum of this Lease (which recording fee shall be at Tenant's sole cost and expense), free and clear of all liens, encumbrances and restrictions, except for those items set forth on Exhibit "C" attached hereto and made a part hereof and any current or future lien to secure financing by the Landlord or any subsequent landlord who acquires fee simple title to the Leased Premises (subject to the requirements of Article 18(d) below; and (4) that upon Tenant paying the rents and keeping the agreements of this Lease on its part to be kept and performed, Tenant shall have peaceful and uninterrupted possession of the entire Leased Premises during the Term of this Lease. Prior to the expiration of the Inspection Period, Landlord shall, at Landlord's expense, furnish to Tenant evidence of Landlord's fee ownership and the recorded status of Landlord's title.

(ii) The existing drive through window and the most recent use of the Building as a drive-through pharmacy do not conform to current Arlington County (Virginia) Zoning Ordinance regulations and are considered legal non conformities. Prior to June 15, 2010, Landlord, at Landlord's expense, shall provide to Tenant written evidence from Arlington County in a form reasonably acceptable to Tenant ("Zoning Evidence") evidencing that the non-conforming structures and previous uses may be continued by the Tenant so long as the use continues and such use is not discontinued for more than one year and so long as the buildings or structures are maintained in their then structural condition and the building or structure is not enlarged. The Zoning Evidence will also evidence that if the Tenant opens the existing drive-through window for business with the public within 90 days from the date a building permit for non-structural alterations to the Building has been issued by Arlington County, and provided such permit is issued on or before April 1, 2010, the previous use of the drive-through will be deemed continued.

(ii) To the extent that Landlord's consent is required or sought with respect to any document now or hereafter encumbering Tenant's leasehold title to the Leased Premises (including, but not limited to any item listed on Exhibit "C" hereto), or to the extent that under any such document under which Landlord has the right and opportunity to cast a vote regarding any matter, any consent or vote of Landlord given absent Tenant's express consent or direction shall be of no effect and deemed invalid. Landlord is hereby obligated to immediately notify Tenant, in writing, of any request for consent or call for a vote under any such encumbering document, and provide Tenant with any correspondence relating thereto. Upon direction from Tenant, Landlord must make its election or cast its vote according to Tenant's instructions pursuant to this Paragraph.

(b) Landlord warrants and represents to Tenant that no recorded encumbrance or restriction imposed upon the Leased Premises, whether or not described in this Article 18(b), shall impair or restrict any right granted to Tenant or derived by Tenant under this Lease, including the right to operate 24 hours per day, seven days per week, and Landlord does hereby indemnify, defend and hold Tenant harmless from and against all claims, actions, damages, loss, cost and expense (including without limitation attorneys fees and court costs) resulting directly or indirectly from the breach of the foregoing warranty and representation.

(c) If as of the date of the recordation of the Memorandum of this Lease, the Leased Premises, or any part thereof, is subject to any mortgage, deed of trust or other encumbrance in the nature of a mortgage, which is prior and superior to this Lease, it is a further express condition hereof that Landlord shall thereupon furnish and deliver to Tenant, a Subordination, Non-Disturbance and Attornment Agreement in substantially the form attached hereto as Exhibit "D" (the "SNDA)..

(d) If required by Landlord's or successor Landlord's institutional lender holding a mortgage lien or deed of trust, Tenant shall provide Landlord the SNDA within 30 days after receipt of written request therefore. Commencing on the thirteenth (13th) month of the Term and prior to the issuance of any subordination by Tenant, Landlord shall pay to Tenant an administrative charge in an amount equal to Five Hundred Dollars ($500.00).

(e) It is understood and agreed that Tenant shall, in no event, be obligated to accept possession of the Leased Premises until the Landlord has complied with the provisions of this Article 18.

REAL ESTATE TAXES

19. (a) Landlord, prior to the commencement of the Term, shall make a mailing address change on the property tax records so that the tax bill and tax notices for only the Leased Premises, when mailed, will be mailed to Tenant on and after the commencement of the Term at the following address: The Drug Store., Attn: Tax Department, P.O. Box 500, Chicago, Illinois 60000. If Landlord fails to cause such address change prior to the Possession Date and if such failure prevents Tenant from contesting any increase in taxes, Landlord shall be solely obligated to pay increases, if any, in such taxes occurring between the date of this Lease and the date that is thirty (30) days after the effective date of such change of address, or increases in such taxes resulting from changes in the assessed value of the Leased Premises occurring between such dates. Prior to the date that the tax bill is mailed directly to Tenant pursuant hereto, Landlord, prior to delinquency, shall send to Tenant a copy of the tax bill for the Leased Premises.

(b) Upon receipt of the aforesaid tax bills, Tenant shall pay, when due and before delinquency, the ad valorem real estate taxes (including all special benefit taxes and special assessments) levied and assessed against the Leased Premises, as of the commencement of the Term and continuing for the remainder of the Term. However, the ad valorem taxes levied or assessed for the year in which Tenant commences paying fixed rent shall be prorated between Landlord and Tenant so that Tenant shall pay only such part thereof as pertains to the period commencing on the beginning of the Term, and the ad valorem taxes levied or assessed for the year during which this Lease expires or is terminated shall be prorated between Landlord and Tenant so that Tenant shall pay only such part thereof as pertains to the period commencing on January 1st and ending on the date this Lease expires or is terminated. In no event shall Tenant be required to pay real estate taxes pertaining to any period prior to the commencement of the Term or subsequent to the expiration or earlier termination of the Lease. Within thirty (30) days of Tenant's request, Landlord shall reimburse Tenant for Tenant's payment of that portion of the tax bill pertaining to any period prior to the commencement of the Term or subsequent to the expiration or early termination of the Term. Within thirty (30) days of Landlord's request, Tenant shall reimburse Landlord for Landlord's payment of that portion of the tax bill pertaining to any period subsequent to the commencement of the Term or prior to the expiration or early termination of the Term.

(c) All special benefit taxes and special assessments shall be spread over the longest time permitted and Tenant's liability for installments of such special benefit taxes and special assessments not yet due shall cease upon the expiration or termination of this Lease. In no event shall Tenant be obligated to pay any impact fees whether or not billed by the taxing authority as a special benefit tax or a special assessment, unless arising from Tenant's improvements or alterations.

(d) (i) Tenant shall have the right to contest the validity or the amount of any tax or assessment levied against the Leased Premises or any improvements thereon, provided that Tenant shall not take any action which will cause or allow the institution of foreclosure proceedings against the Leased Premises. Landlord shall cooperate in the institution of any such proceedings to contest the validity or amount of real estate taxes and will execute any documents required therefore.

(ii) Landlord covenants and agrees that if there shall be any refunds or rebates on account of any tax, governmental imposition or levy paid by Tenant under the provisions of this Lease, such refund or rebate shall belong to Tenant. Any such refunds or rebates received by Landlord shall be held in trust for the benefit of Tenant and shall be forthwith paid to Tenant. Landlord shall, on request of Tenant, sign any receipt which may be necessary to secure the payment of any such refund or rebate, and shall pay over to Tenant such refund or rebate as received by Landlord.

(e) The tax parcel ID number(s) for the Leased Premises are set forth below.

15-012-041 INSURANCE

20. Commencing with the Possession Date and continuing until the last day of the two hundred fortieth (240th) full calendar month of the Term, Tenant shall carry special form coverage insurance covering the Building and the other improvements on the Leased Premises to the extent of not less than 100 percent of replacement value, with companies which are authorized to do business in the State in which the Leased Premises is located and are governed by the regulatory authority which establishes maximum rates in the vicinity. Commencing with the first day of the two hundred forth first (241st) full calendar month of the Term, such coverage shall be on an actual cash value basis. Tenant shall also procure and continue in effect public liability and property damage insurance with respect to the operation of the Leased Premises. Such public liability insurance shall cover liability and property damage for death or bodily injury in any one accident, mishap or casualty in a combined single limit sum of not less than $3,000,000.00. The proceeds from Tenant's casualty insurance hereunder shall be paid and applied only as set forth in Article 14 hereof. Tenant shall name Landlord and/or Landlord's mortgagee as additional insured under such coverage; provided that neither Tenant nor Tenant's insurer (notwithstanding Tenant's self insurance) shall have any obligation to cover or provide protection to Landlord (or its mortgagee) with respect to the alleged acts or omissions of any contractor or subcontractor engaged or permitted by or through Landlord if such contractor or subcontractor does not itself carry insurance for bodily injury, death and property damage in at least the same amounts as Tenant is required to carry hereinabove, with companies which are authorized to do business in the State in which the Leased Premises is located. Any insurance carried or required to be carried by Tenant pursuant to this Lease, at Tenant's option may, be carried under an insurance policy(ies), self-insurance (provided Tenant maintains a net worth of not less than $100,000,000) or pursuant to a master policy of insurance or so-called blanket policy of insurance covering other locations of Tenant or its corporate affiliates, or any combination thereof. Each policy shall provide that coverage cannot be canceled without 30 days prior written notice to Landlord. Promptly upon request, Tenant shall provide Landlord with evidence of all insurance.

MUTUAL INDEMNITY

21. Except for loss, cost and expense caused by fire or other casualty, Landlord and Tenant shall each indemnify, defend and hold harmless the other against and from any and all claims, damages, actions, loss, cost and expense (including but not limited to attorneys fees) resulting directly or indirectly from their own respective negligent acts or omissions or the negligent acts or omissions of their respective employees or agents (acting within the scope of their employment or agency).

BROKERAGE

22. Landlord and Tenant represent that they have dealt with no broker or agent with respect to this Lease, other than Calkain Companies. Landlord hereby indemnifies, defends, saves and holds Tenant harmless against any claims for brokerage commissions or compensation or other claims of any kind (including reasonable attorney's fees) arising out of the negotiation and execution of this Lease or Tenant's interest or involvement with respect to the Leased Premises.

PREVAILING PARTY

23. In the event of litigation between Landlord and Tenant in connection with this Lease, the reasonable attorneys' fees and court costs incurred by the party prevailing in such litigation, including appeals, shall be borne by the non-prevailing party.

NOTICES

24. Except as otherwise expressly provided elsewhere in this Lease, all notices hereunder shall be in writing and sent by United States certified or registered mail, postage prepaid, or by overnight delivery service providing proof of receipt, addressed if to Landlord, to the place where rent checks are to be mailed, with a copy to Ron T. Jones, Esq., Jones Hart Smith s.c., PO Box 350, Green Bay, WI 00000, and if to Tenant, to The Drug Store., Attn: Tax Department, P.O. Box 500, Chicago, Illinois 60000. Attn: Corporate and Transactional Law Department, Real Estate Group, Re: Store #1555, and a duplicate to the Leased Premises, provided that each party by like notice may designate any future or different addresses to which subsequent notices shall be sent. Notices shall be deemed given upon receipt or upon refusal to accept delivery.

RIGHT OF FIRST REFUSAL

25. (a) In the event that Landlord shall receive a Bona Fide Offer to purchase the Leased Premises at any time and from time to time on or after July 1, 2011 and during the remaining Term of this Lease or any extensions thereof from any person or entity, Landlord shall so notify

Tenant (Attn.: Corporate and Transactional Law Department, Real Estate Group) together with a true and correct copy of said Bona Fide Offer. For purposes hereof, a "Bona Fide Offer" shall be deemed to be one made in writing by a person or entity that is not related to or affiliated with Landlord, which Landlord intends to accept (subject to this Article 25). In submitting the Bona Fide Offer to Tenant, Landlord shall segregate the price and the terms of the offer for the Leased Premises from the price and other terms connected with any additional property or properties that such person or entity is offering to purchase from Landlord, such that Tenant may purchase the Leased Premises separate from any such additional property or properties. In no event shall the Bona Fide Offer condition the purchase of the Leased Premises on the purchase of any additional properties from Landlord. Tenant may, at Tenant's option and within twenty-one (21) days after receipt of Landlord's notice of said Bona Fide Offer and receipt of a copy thereof and, if applicable, any relevant loan assumption documentation, offer to purchase the Leased Premises at the price and upon the terms and conditions as are contained in said Bona Fide Offer, in which event, Landlord shall sell the Leased Premises to Tenant upon said terms and conditions and said price; furthermore, in such event, Landlord shall convey the Leased Premises to Tenant by special warranty deed. Notwithstanding the foregoing, the price that Tenant shall pay for the Leased Premises shall be reduced by an amount equal to broker's fees or commissions that would have been payable by Landlord if the Leased Premises were sold pursuant to a Bona Fide Offer. Landlord shall provide Tenant evidence of the amount of broker's fees or commissions payable in connection with any such Bona Fide Offer. Landlord covenants that it shall accept no such Bona Fide Offer (unless such Bona Fide Offer is expressly made subject to Tenant's right of first refusal) or convey the premises until it has complied with the terms of this Article 25. Any conveyance of the Leased Premises made in the absence of full satisfaction of this Article 25 shall be void. Tenant may enforce this Article 25, without limitation, by injunction, specific performance or other equitable relief.

(b) Tenant's election not to exercise its Right of First Refusal shall not prejudice Tenant's rights hereunder as to any further Bona Fide Offer. The terms and conditions contained in this Article 25 shall be binding upon the heirs, successors and assigns of Landlord.

TRANSFER OF TITLE

26. (a) Subject to the provisions of Article 25 above, Landlord may convey its interest in the Leased Premises to any other person or entity. In the event that Landlord conveys its interest in the Leased Premises to any other person or entity, Tenant shall have no obligation to pay rents or any other charges under this Lease to any such transferee until Tenant has been so notified and has received satisfactory evidence of such conveyance together with (i) a written direction from such transferee as to the name and address of the new payee of rents and other charges, (ii) such transferee's FEIN or social security number and (iii) the name and address of the party to receive a 1099 from Tenant. It is understood and agreed that Tenant's withholding of rent and other charges until its receipt of such satisfactory evidence shall not be deemed a default under this Lease.

(b) In the event that Landlord conveys its interest in the Leased Premises, Landlord shall take all measures necessary to cause real estate tax bills and notices to continue to be mailed to Tenant as required under Article 19.

(c) In the event that Landlord conveys its interest in the Leased Premises, the party transferring such interest shall be relieved of all obligations of Landlord arising under this Lease after such transfer, provided the transferee assumes such obligations in writing.

RENT TAX

27. Notwithstanding any provision of Article 19 to the contrary, in the event that any governmental authority imposes a tax, charge, assessment or other imposition upon tenants in general which is based upon the rents payable under this Lease, Tenant shall pay the same to said governmental authority or to Landlord if Landlord is responsible to collect the same (in which case Landlord shall remit the same in a timely manner and, upon request of Tenant, evidence to Tenant said remittance). Nothing contained herein shall be deemed to obligate Tenant with respect to any income, inheritance or successor tax or imposition. Notwithstanding any other provision of this Paragraph, Landlord shall be responsible to pay any so-called "business license tax" (or the like) imposed upon landlords generally in connection with the operation of their business, even if such tax is calculated based upon rents payable under a lease.

AUDIT

28. Tenant reserves the right to inspect and audit at any time, and from time to time, Landlord's books, records and other documents which evidence the purchase price of the land legally described on Exhibit "B". In connection therewith, Landlord shall retain such books, records and other documents that will enable Tenant to conduct such audit. In addition, prior to delivery of possession of the Leased Premises to Tenant, Landlord shall furnish Tenant with a copy of its fully executed closing statement evidencing the purchase price of the land legally described on Exhibit "B" and the last two deeds of record. The foregoing obligations shall expressly survive the assignment of this Lease or sale of the Leased Premises by the person or entity who or which is the Landlord executing this Lease.

ESTOPPEL CERTIFICATE

29. During the Term of the Lease, Landlord and Tenant agree to execute and deliver to the other within thirty (30) days after receipt of such request, an estoppel certificate in form and substance acceptable to the party issuing such certificate, which certificate may include information as to any modification of this Lease, dates of commencement of Term and the termination date of this Lease, and to the best of Landlord's or Tenant's knowledge, whether or not Landlord or Tenant is in default of this Lease. Commencing on the thirteenth (13th) month of the Term and prior to the issuance of any such estoppel certificate by Tenant, Landlord shall pay to Tenant an administrative charge in an amount equal to Five Hundred Dollars ($500.00).

CONDEMNATION

30. (a) If the entire Leased Premises and/or the Building shall be taken by reason of condemnation or under eminent domain proceedings, this Lease shall terminate as of the date when possession of the Leased Premises and/or the Building is so taken, and the rent reserved in this Lease shall be adjusted so that rent is payable only to the date of taking. The total compensation awarded for the Leased Premises and/or Building so taken shall be divided between Landlord and Tenant as follows without any agreement as to the priority of distribution, except as otherwise stated below:

(i) Landlord shall be entitled to a portion of the compensation equal to the present value of the anticipated fixed rent payable pursuant to Article 2(a) above for the unexpired balance of the Term, determined as of the date of such taking.

(ii) Tenant shall be entitled to a portion of the compensation for damage to Tenant's fixtures, equipment, leasehold improvements, other personal property, relocation expenses and for the value of the Tenant's leasehold taken (based on the unexpired balance of the Term as of the date of such taking); and

(iii) Landlord shall be entitled to the balance of such compensation after the distributions set forth in Sections(a)(i) and (a)(ii) above.

(b) If a portion of the Leased Premises and/or Building shall be taken by reason of condemnation or under eminent domain proceedings and if in the opinion of Tenant, reasonably exercised, the remainder of the Leased Premises and/or the Building are no longer suitable for the operation of Tenant's business, and if Landlord has refused to restore the Premises in such manner as is reasonably required by Tenant for the operation of Tenant's business, Tenant may terminate this Lease with notice to Landlord effective as of the date of such taking and any unearned rents and other charges paid or credited in advance of the effective date of such termination shall be refunded to Tenant. Any notice of termination sent by Tenant pursuant to this Section (b) shall be sent to Landlord no later than sixty (60) days after such taking.

(i) If Tenant shall exercise its right to terminate this Lease pursuant to this Section (b) then Tenant shall be entitled to a portion of the compensation to be divided between Landlord and Tenant in the manner set forth in Section (a) above.

(ii) If this Lease is not terminated by Tenant pursuant to Section (b)(i) of this Article, then Tenant shall, at its sole cost and expense, restore the remaining portions of the Leased Premises and/or the Building in the manner Tenant deems necessary or desirable (subject to applicable law) and Tenant shall be entitled to a portion of the total compensation to be divided between Landlord and Tenant as follows: (1) first, to Tenant an amount sufficient for Tenant to restore the Leased Premises and/or the Building, subject to all rights and restrictions of Landlord's lender; and (2) the remainder of the compensation shall be allocated between Landlord and Tenant in the manner set forth in Section (a)(ii) and Section (a)(iii) above; provided that Tenant shall not receive any duplicate compensation (e.g., Tenant shall not be compensated for loss or damage to fixtures, equipment, leasehold improvements, other personal property if Tenant has already been compensated to restore or replace the same items).

(c) Provided that Tenant does not elect to terminate this Lease as above provided, Tenant shall be entitled to any compensation for any temporary construction easements.

(d) If this Lease is terminated under this Article, then Tenant's and Landlord's rights to all or a portion of the compensation under this Paragraph shall survive such termination.

(e) For the purposes of this Article, the term "condemnation or eminent domain proceedings" shall include conveyances and grants made in anticipation of or in lieu of such proceedings.

MISCELLANEOUS

31. (a) Captions of the several Articles contained in this Lease are for convenience only and do not constitute a part of this Lease and do not limit, affect or construe the contents of such Articles.

(b) If any provision of this Lease shall be held to be invalid, illegal or unenforceable, the validity, legality and enforceability of the remaining provisions shall in no way be affected or impaired thereby.

(c) If Landlord is comprised of more than one person or entity, the obligations imposed on Landlord under this Lease shall be joint and several.

(d) All provisions of this Lease have been negotiated by both parties at arm's length and neither party shall be deemed the scrivener of this Lease. This Lease shall not be construed for or against either party by reason of the authorship or alleged authorship of any provision hereof.

(e) This instrument shall merge all undertakings, representations, understandings, and agreements whether oral or written, between the parties hereto with respect to the Leased Premises and the provisions of this Lease and shall constitute the entire Lease unless otherwise hereafter modified by both parties in writing.

(f) This instrument shall also bind and benefit, as the case may require, the heirs, legal representatives, assigns and successors of the respective parties, and all covenants, conditions and agreements herein contained shall be construed as covenants running with the land. This instrument shall not become binding upon the parties until it shall have been executed and delivered by both Landlord and Tenant.

(g) Landlord has been afforded a full and fair opportunity to seek advice from legal counsel and Landlord acknowledges that Tenant's attorney represents Tenant and not Landlord.

(h) Notwithstanding any provision of this Lease to the contrary, the Term shall commence, if at all, not later than twenty-one (21) years after the date of this Lease.

IN WITNESS WHEREOF, Landlord and Tenant have executed this Lease, under seal, as of the day and year first above written.

Tenant: Landlord:

THE DRUG STORE   DAVIS LIMITED PARTNERSHIP

By: By:

Print Name: John M. Smith   Print Name: Robert E. Dwyer

Its: Divisional Vice President   Its: Divisional Vice President

WITNESSES: WITNESSES:

(Notary and exhibit pages follow.)

I, the undersigned, a Notary Public, do hereby certify that John M. Smith, personally known to me to be the Divisional Vice President of THE DRUG STORE, an Illinois corporation, and personally known to me to be the person whose name is subscribed in the foregoing instrument, appeared before me this day in person and acknowledged that he signed and delivered the said instrument as such Divisional Vice President of said corporation, pursuant to authority given by the Board of Directors of said corporation, as his free and voluntary act, and as the free and voluntary act and deed of said corporation, for the purposes therein set forth.

Given under my hand and notarial seal this _____ day of _____, 2010.

My commission expires: _____

     Notary Public

I, a Notary Public, do hereby certify that _____, personally known to me to be the _____ of DAVIS LIMITED PARTNERSHIP, an Illinois limited partnership, and personally known to me to be the person whose name is subscribed in the foregoing instrument, appeared before me this day in person and severally acknowledged that they signed and delivered the said instrument as such _____ of said company, , pursuant to authority given by the members of said company, as his free and voluntary act, and as the free and voluntary act and deed of said company, for the purposes therein set forth.

Given under my hand and notarial seal this _____ day of _____, 2010.

My commission expires: _____

Notary Public

EXHIBIT "A"

SITE PLAN

TO BE ATTACHED

EXHIBIT "B"

LEGAL DESCRIPTION OF LEASED PREMISES

EXHIBIT "C"

PERMITTED TITLE EXCEPTIONS

1.   General ad valorem real estate taxes and assessments not yet due and payable.

2.   Such utility easements as are necessary to supply utility service to the Leased Premises, provided, however, that no easements shall run underneath the Building nor above or immediately adjacent to (and above ground) the Building so as to obstruct visibility of the Building or affect use of the drive through facility. Utility easement areas shall be subject to review and approval by Tenant as part of the Plans under Article 5 and as part of Tenant's title review under Article 18 of the Lease [delete or confirm contingency waived].

3. [Need to list all exceptions shown on new title commitment]

EXHIBIT "D"

Form of SNDA (This Space for Recording Use Only)

THIS DOCUMENT SHOULD BE RETURNED TO AFTER RECORDING:

THE	DRUG	STORE
P.O.	Box	500
Chicago, Illinois 60000		

Attn: Kristin Davidson

Corporate and Transactional Law Department

Real Estate Group - Store # _____

SUBORDINATION, NON-DISTURBANCE AND ATTORNMENT AGREEMENT

THIS SUBORDINATION, NON-DISTURBANCE AND ATTORNMENT AGREEMENT made in multiple copies as of the _____ day of _____, 20__, by and between _____, a(n)_____ ("Mortgagee"), _____, a(n) _____ ("Landlord") and The Drug Store, an Illinois corporation ("Tenant");

WITNESSETH:

WHEREAS, Mortgagee is the holder of a Note in the original principal amount of $_____, secured by a Mortgage or Deed of Trust ("Mortgage") dated _____, 20__, recorded on _____, 20__, in Book _____, at Page _____, in the Official Records of _____, State of _____, covering the property legally described on Exhibit "A" attached hereto and made a part hereof;

WHEREAS, by Lease dated _____, 20__, ("Lease"), recorded by Memorandum of Lease of even date, on _____, 20__, in Book _____, at Page _____, in the Official Records of _____ County, State of _____, Landlord, as landlord, leased to Tenant, as tenant, the property, of the _____ corner of _____ and _____ in _____, _____, legally described on Exhibit "A" ("Leased Premises");

WHEREAS, Mortgagee, Tenant and Landlord desire to confirm their understanding with respect to said Lease and said Mortgage;

NOW, THEREFORE, in consideration of the premises and the mutual covenants and promises contained herein and other good and valuable consideration, the parties agree as follows:

1. Subject to the covenants, terms and conditions of this Agreement, in the event of a default under the Note, the lien of said Lease is hereby subordinated to the lien of said Mortgage. If there shall be a conflict between the terms of said Lease and the terms of said Mortgage, the terms of said Lease shall prevail.

2. In the event Mortgagee or any other party (collectively "Successor Landlord") acquires title or right of possession of the Leased Premises under said Mortgage through foreclosure, or other procedure related to a default under the Note, said Lease shall remain in full force and effect and Tenant shall continue occupancy of the Leased Premises in accordance with the terms and provisions of said Lease. In such event, during the period that it holds title to or possession of the Leased Premises, Successor Landlord shall be in all respects bound by said Lease as Landlord and by all of Tenant's rights thereunder. Successor Landlord's remedies pursuant to the Lease will be in full force and effect once Successor Landlord succeeds to the interest of Landlord under the Lease and once Successor Landlord is bound by all of the terms and conditions of said Lease.

3. So long as Successor Landlord shall be bound by the terms and conditions of said Lease, Tenant shall attorn to Successor Landlord when Successor Landlord is in possession of the Leased Premises, whether such possession is pursuant to Mortgagee's rights under said Mortgage (which such attornment shall be effective and self operative without the execution of

any further instrument on the part of any of the parties hereto), or other procedure related to a default under the Note and will continue occupancy of the Leased Premises under the same terms and conditions of said Lease.

4. Mortgagee shall not include Tenant in any foreclosure proceeding involving the Leased Premises, unless required by applicable state law for Mortgagee to accomplish the foreclosure and then not to interfere with or diminish Tenant's rights under said Lease or disturb Tenant's possession.

5. In the event that Successor Landlord succeeds to the interest of Landlord under such Lease, Successor Landlord shall not be:

a). Liable for any act or omission of any prior landlord (including Landlord) or subject to any offsets or defenses which Tenant might have against any prior landlord (including Landlord), except for any defaults or remedies of which Tenant has notified Mortgagee prior to Successor Landlord becoming bound by the Lease in accordance with paragraph 2. Successor Landlord will not be held liable for any consequential damages for defaults of any prior Landlord; or b). Bound by any payment of any rent or additional rent which Tenant might have paid for more than the current month to any prior landlord (including Landlord); or c) Bound by any amendment or modification of the Lease made without Mortgagee's written consent.

6. During the continuance of said Mortgage, Tenant shall use reasonable efforts to give written notice to Mortgagee of all defaults by Landlord of those obligations under said Lease which are of a nature as to give Tenant a right to terminate said Lease, reduce rent, or to credit or offset any amounts against future rents, and Mortgagee shall have the same opportunity as provided to Landlord in said Lease (but shall not be required) to cure the same. In any event (except as otherwise provided in the next sentence of this paragraph), Tenant's failure to provide Mortgagee such written notice shall not impair any rights granted or derived by Tenant under said Lease and/or this Agreement. In no event shall Tenant terminate the Lease as a result of any breach or default of the Lease unless Tenant has provided Mortgagee notice and afforded the Mortgagee the same opportunity to cure such breach or default as provided to Landlord in said Lease; provided, however, that Mortgagee shall not be obligated to remedy or cure any default of Landlord under the Lease.

7. Tenant hereby agrees that upon receipt of written notice from Mortgagee of a default by Landlord under said Mortgage, all checks for rent and other sums payable by Tenant under said Lease to Landlord shall, from the date of Tenant's receipt of such written notice, be delivered to and drawn to the exclusive order of Mortgagee until Mortgagee or a court of competent jurisdiction shall direct otherwise. Such an assignment of rent shall not relieve Landlord of any of its obligations under said Lease and shall not modify or diminish any rights granted to Tenant by said Lease or this Agreement, including but not limited to, any rights contained in said Lease which allow Tenant the right of so-called self help, offsets or deductions in the event of default or otherwise. Landlord hereby consents and agrees to the provisions of this paragraph and hereby authorizes Tenant to direct all rental and other payments under said Lease as provided by this paragraph. Landlord hereby relieves Tenant from any liability by reason of Tenant's payment of any sums under said Lease as required by this paragraph. Tenant shall have no obligation to verify the existence of any such default stated in the notice from Mortgagee under this paragraph.

8. (a) Subject to the terms of (b) below, Tenant agrees that the covenants of Landlord in Article ____ of the Lease shall not be binding upon land owned by Successor Landlord that acquires the

interest of Landlord in the Leased Premises through foreclosure of the Mortgage or a deed in lieu thereof, (provided that Successor Landlord owned or mortgaged such land prior to the date that it acquires the interest of Landlord in the Leased Premises), but shall apply to any subsequent purchaser or transferee that is not an affiliate or subsidiary of Successor Landlord.

(b) Upon Successor Landlord's acquisition of Landlord's interest, during the period that it holds title to the Leased Premises, Successor Landlord will not execute any agreement that violates the restrictions set forth in Article _____ of the Lease or agree to any modification of a then existing agreement which extends the right of any third party to operate in a manner inconsistent with the restrictions set forth in Article ___ of the Lease.

1.   In the event Successor Landlord acquires title or right of possession of the Leased Premises, Tenant acknowledges and agrees that the liability of such Successor Landlord under the Lease shall be limited to its interest in the property described on Exhibit "A" and the rents, income and profits therefrom. Notwithstanding anything herein to the contrary, Tenant shall have all of its equitable remedies against Successor Landlord. Nothing contained herein shall otherwise limit Tenant's rights or remedies as provided in the Lease.

2.   All notices under this Agreement shall be deemed to have been duly given if made in writing and sent by United States certified or registered mail, postage prepaid, or by overnight delivery service providing proof of receipt, and addressed as follows:

If to Mortgagee: If to Tenant: P.O. Box 500, Chicago, Illinois 60000. If to Landlord: 100 Main Street Suite 20 Barrington, Illinois 60010. Provided that each party by like notice may designate any future or different addresses to which subsequent notices shall be sent. Notices shall be deemed given upon receipt or upon refusal to accept delivery.

1.   Tenant agrees that the right of first refusal shall not apply to Successor Landlord through a foreclosure, deed-in-lieu of foreclosure or any other enforcement action under the Mortgage; provided, however, such right of first refusal shall apply to subsequent purchasers of the Leased Premises. It is the express intention of Landlord and Tenant that the acquisition by either party of the right, title, interest and estate of the other party in and to the Leased Premises shall not result in termination or cancellation of the Lease by operation of the principle of merger of estates or otherwise, notwithstanding any applicable law to the contrary.

2.   To facilitate execution, this Agreement may be executed in as many counterparts as may be convenient or required. It shall not be necessary that the signature and acknowledgment of, or on behalf of, each party, or that the signature and acknowledgment of all persons required to bind any party, appear on each counterpart. All counterparts shall collectively constitute a single instrument. It shall not be necessary in making proof of this Agreement to produce or account for more than a single counterpart containing the respective signatures and acknowledgment of, or on behalf of, each of the parties hereto. Any signature and acknowledgment page to any counterpart may be detached from such counterpart without impairing the legal effect of the signatures and acknowledgments thereon and thereafter attached to another counterpart identical thereto except having attached to it additional signature and acknowledgment pages.

3.   This Agreement shall also bind and benefit the heirs, legal representatives, successors and assigns of the respective parties hereto, and all covenants, conditions and agreements herein contained shall be construed as running with the land.

IN WITNESS WHEREOF, the parties hereto have executed and delivered this Agreement, under seal, as of the day and year first above written.

(Signature Page to follow)

THE DRUG STORE, MORTGAGEE

John M. Smith By:

Divisional Vice President Title:

LANDLORD (Enter name here)

By: Title:

PLEASE ATTACH LEGAL DESCRIPTION FOR EXECUTION OF DOCUMENT

EXHIBIT "A" LEGAL DESCRIPTION (STORE #_____)

ACKNOWLEDGEMENT

STATE OF ILLINOIS

COUNTY OF LAKE

On this _____ day of _____ 20 , before me appeared John M. Smith, to me personally known, who, being by me duly sworn, did say that he is the Divisional Vice President of The Drug Store, an Illinois corporation, and that said instrument was signed in behalf of said corporation by authority of its board of directors, and said Divisional Vice President acknowledged said instrument to be the free act and deed of said corporation.

(Seal) _____

Notary Public My term expires:

Appendix B

Sample Ground Lease

DEED OF GROUND LEASE

THIS DEED OF GROUND LEASE (this "Lease"), dated as of the later of the dates accompanying the signatures by Landlord and Tenant, is by and between NT PARTNERS, LLC , a Virginia limited liability company ("Landlord"), and AMERICA'S BANK, N.A., a national banking association ("Tenant"), who agree as follows:

1. PREMISES. Landlord hereby leases to Tenant, and Tenant hereby leases from Landlord for the term, at the rental and upon the conditions set forth below, that certain parcel of real property containing approximately 1.50 acres of land (the "Land") in the shopping center known as Turner Square Shopping Center (the "Shopping Center"), located at the southwest corner of Main Street (Route 2) and Turner Road (Route 650) in Monroe County, Virginia, as more fully described on Exhibit "A" attached hereto and shown on the "Site Plan" depicted on Exhibit "A-1" also attached hereto and incorporated herein by this reference, together with all rights, privileges, easements and appurtenances belonging or in any way pertaining to the Land, and any improvements presently on the Land (if any), being hereinafter referred to as the "Premises."

2. TERM. The term of this Lease (the "Lease Term" or "Term") shall commence at 12:01

a.m. on the date which this Lease is signed by both Landlord and Tenant (the "Commencement Date") and shall end at 11:59 pm on that date (the "Expiration Date") that is the last day of the month in which the twenty-fifth (25th) anniversary of the Rent Commencement Date (as defined in Section 7.2 below) occurs, provided that such Expiration Date shall be automatically extended to the last day of any Renewal Term following Tenant's delivery of its Extension Notice to Landlord (as defined in Section 3 below) for such Renewal Term, unless the Lease Term shall be terminated earlier in accordance with the terms hereof.

3. OPTION TO RENEW. Landlord hereby grants to Tenant the right to renew the term of this Lease for five (5) additional separate, consecutive five (5) year periods (each a "Renewal Term"), subject to all of the same terms and conditions contained herein, and provided that at the time for each exercise of Tenant's option to renew, Tenant is not in material default beyond any applicable notice and cure periods (as provided in Section 21.1) of any of the covenants or agreements contained in this Lease to be performed by Tenant. Tenant's respective options to renew shall be exercised, if at all (i.e., and if not so exercised, shall be deemed waived), by Tenant's giving to Landlord notice in writing of such exercise (the "Extension Notice") not later than one hundred eighty (180) days prior to the then-existing Expiration Date of this Lease (the "Extension Notice Deadline").

4. DELIVERY OF PREMISES, CONSTRUCTION AGREEMENT AND OWNERSHIP OF IMPROVEMENTS.

140

4.1 Delivery of Possession. The "Premises Delivery Date" shall be the date on which Landlord has delivered possession of the Premises to Tenant with all of Landlord's Work (as defined below) completed. In no event shall the Premises Delivery Date occur unless and until there is lawful, sufficient ingress and egress for the Premises. If the Premises Delivery Date has not occurred by December 31, 2008, then either Landlord or Tenant shall have the right (but not the obligation) to terminate this Lease by delivering written notice to the other party of such election to terminate this Lease in which event this Lease shall automatically terminate and thereafter neither party shall have any further rights or obligations hereunder.

4.2 Landlord's Work. Prior to the Premises Delivery Date, Landlord shall complete "Landlord's Work" as set forth in the "Construction Agreement" attached hereto as Exhibit "B" and incorporated herein by this reference. The cost of Landlord's Work shall be borne solely by Landlord and shall not be included in Common Area Maintenance Fee (as defined in Section 8).

4.3 Tenant's Work. Tenant shall construct on the Land a retail bank branch building and related improvements, including drive-through teller and automated teller machine ("ATM") lane(s), sidewalks, lighting and landscaping (collectively, the "Building") as described in the "Approved Plans" (as defined in the Construction Agreement). Landlord agrees that Tenant shall be entitled to install its prototypical signage on the exterior of the Building and other improvements constructed on the Premises, at Tenant's sole cost and expense, subject to Landlord's approval, which approval shall not be unreasonably withheld, conditioned or delayed, and further subject to local ordinances. The construction of the Building by Tenant shall be at Tenant's sole cost and expense in accordance with the terms and conditions set forth in the Construction Agreement.

4.4 Ownership of Improvements. The Building and any other improvements of any kind or nature (including, but not limited to, fixtures, equipment and other materials or items) that may be placed upon, installed in or attached to the Premises by Tenant shall, for all purposes, be the property of and assets of Tenant. Tenant shall be solely entitled to any rights or benefits associated with its ownership of the Building and such improvements, fixtures, equipment and other materials or items, including, but not limited to, any depreciation, tax credits or other tax benefits. Notwithstanding the foregoing, the Building and improvements, excluding any removable personal property and Tenant's Business Equipment (as defined in Section 14), shall remain on the Premises after the termination of this Lease and shall thereupon become the property of Landlord.

5. CONDITIONS PRECEDENT TO TENANT'S OBLIGATION TO LEASE THE PREMISES.

(a) As of the date of this Agreement, Tenant shall have the right to obtain, at Tenant's expense, (i) a Title Report issued by a title company licensed in the Commonwealth of Virginia (the "Title Report"), and (ii) a current ALTA survey of the Premises, prepared by a surveyor registered in the Commonwealth of Virginia, which shall overlay all improvements, identify all exceptions listed in the title commitment and any other matters that affect the Premises, and contain a certificate of the square feet in the Premises (the "Survey"). Tenant shall have one hundred (100) days from the date of execution of this Lease by both Landlord and Tenant within which (i) to review all matters contained in the title report and identified on the survey and (ii) to inspect the Premises and conduct such engineering, environmental and other tests of the Premises as Tenant deems advisable (the "Review and Inspection Period"). If Tenant determines, in its sole and absolute discretion, that the Premises are for any reason unacceptable, Tenant may so notify Landlord in writing prior to the expiration of the Review and Inspection Period and may terminate this Lease, and neither party shall have any further rights or obligations hereunder. With respect to such Review and Inspection Period:

(i) Tenant covenants and agrees to indemnify, defend, and hold harmless Landlord from and against all claims, damages and costs incurred by Landlord (including Landlord's reasonable attorneys' fees) as a result of Tenant's access to the Premises for the purposes of conducting said review and inspection of the Premises.

(ii) Any information obtained by Tenant in connection with the Premises shall be considered confidential in nature and not be disclosed by Tenant to any outside third parties.

(iii) In the event Tenant terminates this Lease during the Review and Inspection Period, Tenant shall, within a reasonable period of time after notification to Landlord, return all items to Landlord delivered to Tenant pursuant to Section 5(b) of this Agreement, and also deliver to Landlord copies of any inspections performed by Tenant.

(b) Landlord will deliver upon execution of this Lease by Landlord true and correct copies of all environmental reports, engineering reports, soils tests, permits, reports, copies of existing title policies or commitments and surveys and copies of any existing agreements regarding easements, covenants and restrictions (whether executed, recorded or in draft form) or similar documents pertaining to the Premises, if any, which Landlord has in its possession as well as any other documents as Tenant may reasonably request pertaining to the Premises which Landlord has in its possession; and shall not enter into any leases, encumbrances or other arrangements of any kind whatsoever pertaining to the Premises without the prior written consent of Tenant, which consent shall not be unreasonably withheld, conditioned or delayed.

(c) After obtaining the special use permit as provided in Section 5(d) below, the Land shall be zoned to permit Tenant to use the Premises for a Banking Use (as defined in Section 5(g) below). All costs incurred in connection with such zoning shall be borne solely by Landlord, except as set forth in Section 5(d) below.

(d) Landlord shall apply for and use all commercially reasonable efforts to obtain the special use permit necessary to permit Tenant's Banking Use with drive thru lanes. Landlord and Tenant shall share the cost of obtaining such special use permit equally. Notwithstanding anything to the contrary in this Lease, Tenant shall obtain and pay for Tenant's site and building permits.

(e) Landlord shall cooperate (at no cost to Landlord) with Tenant in applying for and obtaining all of the approvals from various governmental agencies which are necessary for Tenant to construct the Building and operate its intended business from the Premises, including, without limitation, if necessary, signing any such applications or other documents. Tenant agrees to promptly apply for all such approvals and shall use its commercially reasonable best efforts to obtain such approvals. All applications shall be in the form required by the appropriate governmental entity and shall include the payment of all fees. If such approvals have not been obtained by the later of: (x) Landlord's completion of Landlord's Work, or (y) one hundred twenty (120) days after Landlord's approval of the

Final Plans (as described in the Construction Agreement), then Tenant may elect to terminate this Lease pursuant to Section 5(h) below.

(f) Landlord further represents and warrants to Tenant that to the best of Landlord's actual knowledge the Shopping Center and the Premises are in full compliance with all state, federal and local laws, ordinances and regulations (including all environmental regulations), and Tenant's proposed use of the Premises will not violate any such laws.

(g) Landlord further represents and warrants to Tenant that as of the Commencement Date there are no other financial institutions (as hereinafter defined) located in the Restricted Area as shown on Exhibit "A-1" currently conducting retail or wholesale banking operations, which include, but are not limited to, receiving deposits or making loans to the general public, whether done by a state bank, national bank, savings and loan institution, credit union, or other entity (each a "financial institution") and whether accomplished by means of full service, express service, or motorbank facilities, automated teller machines or other self-service banking devices or otherwise (all of the above being hereinafter collectively referred to as the "Banking Use") and further represents that to the best of Landlord's actual knowledge, Tenant's proposed use is not in violation of any covenants, recorded or otherwise, related to the Premises, including any covenants contained in another third party tenant's lease.

(h) In the event all items listed in Sections 5(b) through 5(e) have not been completed or satisfied by the expiration of the Review and Inspection Period, or, if later, the latest date specified for the completion or satisfaction of such item, then Landlord or Tenant may terminate this Lease for a period of fifteen (15) days thereafter by delivering written notice of such termination to the other party in which event this Lease shall automatically terminate and thereafter neither party shall have any further rights or obligations hereunder. Provided, however, that the Landlord may extend this period for up to ninety (90) days by written notice to Tenant. If neither party gives notice of the termination of this Lease within the time period required in this Section 5(h), the right to terminate shall be null and void and this Lease shall remain in full force and effect.

6. USE.

(a) The Premises may be used and occupied by Tenant (and its assignees and subtenants) for the Banking Use and related uses, general business office purposes and any retail, commercial or other lawful use consistent with the operation of a first class shopping center and not in conflict with any restrictions of record or then existing exclusives affecting the Land and parking associated therewith. In no event shall Tenant use the Premises for any use listed on Exhibit "D" attached hereto or commit, or suffer to be committed, any waste upon the Premises.

(b) For the Term of this Lease, Tenant shall be entitled to the use of thirty-five (35) parking spaces on the Land, at the location depicted on Exhibit "A-1", which parking shall be reserved for the exclusive use of Tenant, its customers, invitees, agents and employees (the "Parking Spaces"). The Parking Spaces shall be in compliance with all applicable laws, ordinances, building codes, regulations and other requirements, including without limitation, all requirements of the Americans with Disabilities Act and state and local disabled access laws.

(c) Tenant is not required to occupy the Premises or conduct any business therein and neither failure to occupy or operate on the Premises, nor vacation of the Premises by Tenant shall be a default or breach of this Lease as long as Tenant continues to pay all sums as required hereby and continues to meet all of its other lease obligations. If Tenant discontinues business operations from the Premises, other than as a result of a remodeling, repair, casualty, condemnation or Force Majeure (as defined in Section 42), for more than three hundred sixty (360) days, Landlord shall have the right to terminate this Lease on 30 days' prior written notice to Tenant, provided that such termination shall be conditioned upon Landlord's paying Tenant an amount equal to the unamortized costs (based upon straight line amortization over the initial twenty-five (25) year Term) of the then existing Building and other improvements located on the Premises calculated as of the date of such termination. Notwithstanding the foregoing, if after Landlord sends such termination notice and before the expiration of such 30 day period, Tenant reoccupies the Premises and resumes a permitted use thereof, then this Lease shall not be terminated.

(d) Tenant may, at its own expense, install its own security system in the Premises and/or hire its own security guards to protect the Premises and Tenant's employees, customers and other invitees. Tenant shall be solely responsible, at Tenant's sole expense, for the monitoring, operation and removal of such security system and/or the supervising of any such security guards. Any security system installed or any security guards hired by Tenant will be for the sole benefit of Tenant and its employees, customers and other invitees and Landlord will have no right to rely on any such security systems or guards.

(e) Subject to applicable law and any covenants, conditions and restrictions applicable to the Premises, and Landlord's approval, which shall not be unreasonably withheld, conditioned or delayed; Tenant, at its sole cost and expense, shall have the right to install and maintain its standard corporate signage on the Premises, including, without limitation, (i) a free-standing monument sign, (ii) wall signs on the four (4) sides of the Building; (iii) illuminated signs as part of Tenant's ATMs; (iv) door decals and signs used in the ordinary course of the banking business; and (v) professionally prepared and first class banners and signs in the windows of the Building. Notwithstanding anything to the contrary set forth above, Landlord's consent shall not be required in the event of a change in the name, logo or color of such signage consistent with Tenant's corporate standard (provided that the size, location and quantity of existing signage is not altered) or for signs which are required by law or regulation, provided further that in each instance Tenant shall comply with all Laws (as hereinafter defined) and Landlord's design standards.

(f) Tenant shall have the right to make at any time any alterations, additions or improvements to the interior of the Premises as Tenant deems reasonable in its sole discretion without Landlord's prior written consent (and without the payment of any additional rent), provided that such alterations, additions or improvements shall not reduce the value of the Premises and shall be in compliance with all applicable laws, regulations and ordinances. Any alteration or improvement made to the Premises shall be made in a good and workmanlike manner.

(g) Tenant will be provided access to the Premises twenty-four (24) hours per day, seven days per week. During the Term of this Lease, Tenant, without additional charge unless otherwise expressly provided herein, is entitled to all of the rights and appurtenances applicable to the Premises.

7. RENT.

144

7.1 Rental. As rental (the "Rental") for the Premises during the initial Lease

Term, it is the agreement of the parties that commencing on the Rent Commencement Date Tenant shall pay to Landlord the following sums:

Period	Rentals
Years 1 - 5	$21,250.00 per month
Years 6 - 10	$23,375.00 per month
Years 11 - 15	$25,712.50 per month
Years 16 - 20	$28,283.75 per month
Years 21-25	$31,112.13 per month

7.2 Rental Payments and Rent Commencement Date. The payment of Rental shall commence on the date (the "Rent Commencement Date"), subject to any adjustments pursuant to Section 7(a) of the Construction Agreement, which is the earlier of (a) one hundred fifty (150) days after Landlord's delivery of the Premises to Tenant and the receipt by Tenant of the governmental approvals provided for in Section 5(e) above, or (b) the date Tenant opens for business to the public at the Premises. Rental shall be payable on the first day of each month in advance; provided, however, that in the event that the Rent Commencement Date should occur on a day other than the first day of the month, then the Rental shall be prorated accordingly with such prorated portion being paid on the Rent Commencement Date. Rental for the final month of this Lease shall likewise be prorated if the Expiration Date (or earlier termination date) occurs on other than the final day of a calendar month. The Rental shall be payable, without demand or offset, in lawful money of the United States to Landlord at the address herein provided or at any address designated by Landlord in writing to Tenant. As used herein, the term "Lease Year" means each successive twelve calendar month period, with the first such period commencing on the Rent Commencement Date; provided, however, that if the Rent Commencement Date occurs on a date other than the first day of a month, then the first Lease Year shall commence on the Rent Commencement Date and shall end on the last day of the twelfth calendar month after the Rent Commencement Date and each successive Lease Year shall commence on each anniversary date of the first day of the first calendar month after the Rent Commencement Date (e.g., if Rent Commencement Date is March 20, the first Lease Year shall end on March 31 of the following year and each successive Lease Year shall commence on April 1). The obligation to pay Rental is an independent covenant. Time is of the essence.

7.3 Rental During Renewal Terms. Tenant shall pay Rental to Landlord for the Premises during the Renewal Terms in the following sums:

Period	Monthly Rental
1st Renewal Term	$34,223.34 per month

2nd Renewal Term	$37,645.67 per month
3rd Renewal Term	$41,410.24 per month
4th Renewal Term	$45,551.26 per month
5th Renewal Term	$50,106.39 per month

8. COMMON AREA MAINTENANCE FEE. In addition to the Rental payable pursuant to Section 7, Tenant's rental obligation also includes the payment of an off-site common area maintenance fee equal to $0.05 per square foot of the area of the Land for the first Lease Year plus an administrative fee equal to ten percent (10 percent) of the amount otherwise payable (the "Common Area Maintenance Fee"). Such charge shall increase each Lease Year by an amount equal to three percent (3 percent) of the charge for the prior Lease Year. For purposes of this Lease, Tenant's off-site common area maintenance fee and all other charges payable by Tenant under this Lease are "Additional Rent."

Beginning on the Rent Commencement Date, Tenant shall pay to Landlord on the first day of each month in advance, one twelfth (1/12th) of the Additional Rent for each calendar year.

9. TAXES.

(a) Taxes and Assessments. In addition to the rent and any other charges provided for herein, Tenant agrees to pay on demand at the times set forth below, all taxes, assessments, and any other impositions or charges which may be taxes, and are payable from and after the Rent Commencement Date and during the Term of this Lease upon all or any portion of the Premises, and the improvements on the Premises. Landlord and Tenant shall use reasonable efforts to cause the tax bills to be sent directly to Tenant from the tax collector and to cause the Premises to be assessed separately and apart from any other land or improvements if this is not already the case. If and to the extent that Landlord and Tenant are not able to cause tax bills to be sent directly to Tenant, Landlord agrees to forward to Tenant, within twenty (20) days after receipt by Landlord, each tax bill, notice of assessment or valuation, and other notice regarding taxes or assessments pertaining to the Premises. During the Term of this Lease, Tenant shall have the right to control any reassessment of the Premises for taxes. Tenant may at its option pay any tax, assessment or other imposition in installments to the extent permitted by applicable law. Tenant shall pay the real property taxes not later than ten (10) days before the taxing authority's delinquency date and shall furnish Landlord with evidence of such payment. If Tenant shall fail to pay any such taxes, assessments or other charges, Landlord shall have the right to pay the same, in which case Tenant shall reimburse Landlord for such amount paid by Landlord within thirty (30) days of written notice to Tenant of Landlord's payment thereof, together with any late charge, interest and/or penalties paid by Landlord. The covenants and agreements to pay taxes by Tenant shall not be deemed to include the payment of any excise, franchise, corporation, income or profit tax, or any municipal, county, state, federal or other gift, estate, succession, inheritance, or transfer taxes of the Landlord or capital levy that is or may be imposed on Landlord. At the commencement and expiration of the Term of this Lease, taxes must be paid by Tenant under this Lease shall be apportioned, and Landlord shall pay that portion thereof applicable to the period before the Rent Commencement Date and after the expiration (or earlier termination) of the Term hereof (as may be extended).

146

(b) Personal Property Taxes. Tenant shall pay before delinquency all taxes, assessments, license fees, and other charges that are levied and assessed against Tenant's personal property installed or located in or on the Premises and that become payable during the Term hereof. If any taxes on Tenant's personal property are levied against Landlord or Landlord's property and if Landlord pays the taxes on any of these items, Tenant, within thirty (30) days of receipt of a detailed invoice therefore, shall immediately reimburse Landlord the sum of the taxes levied on Tenant's personal property against Landlord.

(c) Contest. Tenant, at its sole expense, shall have the right, at any time, to seek a reduction in the assessed valuation of the Premises, and the improvements on the Premises, or to contest any taxes, which are to be paid by Tenant. Landlord shall be required to join in any proceeding or contest brought by or in the name of the Landlord or any owner of the Premises as long as Landlord is not required to bear any cost or liability. The institution of any proceedings or contests, however, shall not release Tenant from paying any real property taxes, assessments, or other charges required to be paid by Tenant hereunder but Tenant may defer payment pending the contest, if and to the extent permitted by applicable law without subjecting the Land to the possibility of foreclosure by the taxing authority.

Landlord agrees to cooperate with Tenant with respect to all real property taxes, assessments or other charges in connection with the Premises, or improvements on the Premises, provided that Tenant shall give written notice to Landlord of any tax proceeding or contest and shall indemnify and hold harmless Landlord from and against any claims, liabilities, lawsuits or damages that may arise in connection with any such proceeding or contest. Any resulting refund shall be applied and paid first to reimburse Tenant for the costs and expenses of the contest, then to Tenant to the extent the refunded tax or assessment was paid by Tenant, and the balance, if any, to Landlord.

1. OFF-SITE COMMON AREA MAINTENANCE. Landlord shall maintain all off-site common areas of the Shopping Center serving the Premises, including all roadways (to the extent not maintained by a public authority) and storm water drainage systems.

2. COMPLIANCE WITH LAWS. Tenant shall comply with, all present and future municipal, county, state, federal and other applicable governmental entities' laws, rules, ordinances and requirements which are now in force, or which may hereafter be in force (collectively "Laws"), that are applicable to the Premises.

3. MAINTENANCE OF PREMISES. Throughout the Lease Term Tenant, at its sole expense, shall maintain all portions of the Premises and all improvements located thereon in good condition, ordinary wear and tear excepted, and in compliance with all Laws. Tenant shall make all repairs and replacements as and when necessary or as required to comply with the foregoing, and all replacements shall be of a quality at least equal to that of the item being replaced. Tenant, at its sole expense, shall at all times keep the Premises reasonably orderly, neat, safe, clean and free from snow, ice, rubbish, dirt and vermin. Tenant shall not burn any trash or garbage at any time in or about the Premises.

4. ALTERATIONS AND ADDITIONS. Tenant shall have the right to make at any time any alterations, additions, or improvements to the interior of the Premises as Tenant deems reasonable, in its sole discretion, without the prior written consent of Landlord and

without the payment of any additional rent, provided that such alterations, additions or improvements shall not reduce the value of the Premises. Tenant shall not make any alterations, additions or improvements to the exterior of the Premises without Landlord's prior written consent, which consent shall not be unreasonably withheld, conditioned or delayed. Except as provided in Sections 4.4 and 14, all alterations, additions and improvements which may be made or installed upon the Premises shall remain upon and be surrendered with the Premises and become the property of Landlord upon the expiration or earlier termination of this Lease. Any alteration or improvement made to the Premises shall be made in a good and workmanlike manner and in compliance with all Laws.

5.   EQUIPMENT, FIXTURES AND SIGNS. Tenant shall have the right to erect, install, maintain and operate on, and remove from, the Premises such equipment, trade and business fixtures, signs and other personal property as Tenant may deem necessary or appropriate (together, "Tenant's Business Equipment"), including but not limited to the following, whether or not installed so as to be fixtures under applicable law: safe deposit boxes, vault doors, automated teller machines and other self-service banking devices, drive-in window systems, undercounter steel, telephone and other communications systems and equipment (including any antennae and related equipment for sending and receiving wireless data and communication information), security systems, computer systems and printers and other computer-related equipment, furniture, furnishings, books, files and records, and such shall not be deemed to be part of the Premises, but shall, subject to Section 27, remain the property of Tenant (i.e., unless left on the Premises for more than thirty (30) days after the termination of this Lease, in which event all such items shall be deemed abandoned by Tenant and shall become the property of Landlord). The Landlord shall not be liable for, and Tenant hereby waives all claims for, any damage to person, property of the Tenant or any other party located on the Premises or for the loss of such property, including consequential damages, except for claims resulting from the gross negligence of Landlord. All property of Tenant kept or stored on the Premises shall be kept or stored at the sole risk of Tenant and the Tenant shall hold the Landlord harmless from any claims arising out of damage to such property, unless caused by the negligence or intentional misconduct of Landlord.

15. ASSIGNMENT AND SUBLETTING.

(a) Tenant may assign this Lease or sublet the whole or any part of the Premises (collectively a "Transfer"), without the prior written consent of Landlord, to any Affiliated Entity, as hereinafter defined. "Affiliated Entity" for purposes of this provision is defined as (a) any entity which controls, is controlled by, or is under common control of Tenant (including a partnership in which Tenant or an affiliate of Tenant is a partner), (b) any entity that succeeds to Tenant's business by merger, consolidation, reorganization or other form of corporate reorganization, (c) any purchaser who acquires all or substantially all of Tenant's assets and/or stock, or (d) any purchaser of substantially all of Tenant's assets in the Commonwealth of Virginia . Otherwise, Tenant shall not consummate a Transfer with any other third party without the prior written consent of Landlord, which consent shall not be unreasonably withheld, conditioned or delayed. Landlord's failure to either approve or disapprove a Transfer within thirty (30) days of Tenant's request for Landlord's consent, shall be deemed to be Landlord's consent of such Transfer. If Landlord timely disapproves a proposed Transfer, then Landlord shall deliver to Tenant a statement of its reasons for objecting to the proposed Transfer.

(b) No assignment or subletting or collection of rent from the assignee or subtenant shall be deemed to constitute a novation or in any way release Tenant, from further performance of

148

its obligations under this Lease; and Tenant, shall continue to be liable under this Lease for the balance of the primary Term and any Renewal Term the option for which was exercised by Tenant or included in the assignment by Tenant, with the same force and effect as if no such assignment had been made, unless otherwise released by Landlord in writing. Landlord's consent to one Transfer shall not be deemed consent to any subsequent proposed Transfer (even if to the same transferee).

16. UTILITY CHARGES. Tenant agrees to pay before delinquency all charges for any utilities furnished to and used by Tenant at the Premises, including, but not limited to, water, electricity, gas, telephone, rubbish, and sewage disposal.

17. INSURANCE. (a) Tenant shall insure the Premises against loss or damage by fire and other casualties included in the so-called "All-Risk Extended Coverage Endorsement" in an amount not less than one hundred percent (100 percent) of the replacement value thereof.

(b) Tenant shall also insure against property damage and public liability arising by reason of occurrences on or about the Premises in the amount of not less than $500,000 in respect of loss or damage to property, in the amount of not less than $2,000,000 in respect of injury to or death of any one person, and in the amount of not less than $4,000,000 in respect of any one accident or disaster.

(c) It is agreed and understood that the insurance coverages provided for herein may be maintained pursuant to master policies of insurance covering other locations of Tenant or its corporate affiliates. All insurance policies required to be maintained by Tenant hereunder shall name Landlord (and, if requested by Landlord, Landlord's mortgagee) as a loss payee or an additional insured, as appropriate. All insurance required by this Section 17 shall be evidenced by certificates issued by insurers licensed in the Commonwealth of Virginia. Tenant shall deliver to Landlord certificates for all such insurance at least thirty (30) days before the expiration of each such insurance policy.

(d) Notwithstanding any other provision of this Lease, Tenant shall have the right to assume in whole or in part, without insurance, any and all risks otherwise required by this Lease to be insured against by Tenant so long as Tenant's net worth is at least $50,000,000.00.

(e) Anything in this Lease to the contrary notwithstanding, Landlord and Tenant each hereby waives any claim it ("Injured Party") may now or hereafter have (and to the extent permitted by applicable law, any claim any of its insurers may now or hereafter have based on subrogation or an assignment from its insured) against the other or the other's directors, officers, employees or agents (each a "Released Party"), for loss of or damage to any of Injured Party's property located in or constituting a part or all of the Building, the Premises, or the Shopping Center, now or hereafter occurring, EVEN IF THE LOSS OR DAMAGE IS CAUSED BY THE NEGLIGENCE OF ANY RELEASED PARTY, OR IF ANY RELEASED PARTY IS STRICTLY LIABLE FOR THE LOSS OR DAMAGE, if the loss or damage is covered by insurance, or if the loss or damage could have been covered by the terms of customary all-risk replacement cost property insurance in the state where the Property is located, in each case without regard to the amount of deductible or the amount of proceeds, if any, and whether or not either or both of Landlord and Tenant have any property insurance.

18. DAMAGE BY FIRE OR OTHER CASUALTY. If any portion of the Premises or any improvements erected thereon, if any, should be destroyed or damaged by fire or other casualty, rent shall not abate and Tenant shall immediately rebuild or repair any such damage at Tenant's sole cost and expense, to at least equal to the value of the same immediately prior to the casualty. All insurance proceeds payable under any property insurance policies covering the Premises (including any improvements located thereon) shall be paid to Tenant to be applied to the cost of repair. Notwithstanding the foregoing, the following shall apply during the last three (3) years of the Lease Term. If, during the last three (3) years of the Lease Term, any portion of the Premises or any improvements erected thereon, if any, should be destroyed or damaged by fire or other casualty, Tenant shall immediately deliver written notice thereof to Landlord and may, at Tenant's sole discretion, commence to rebuild or repair any such damage at Tenant's sole cost and expense. In no event shall Tenant be required to rebuild any damaged improvements during the last three (3) years of the Lease Term. If Tenant elects to rebuild or repair such damage, all insurance proceeds payable under any property insurance policies covering the Premises (including any improvements located thereon) shall be paid to Tenant to be applied to the cost of repair. If Tenant elects to not rebuild the improvements then Landlord may elect to terminate this Lease in which case this Lease would terminate and Landlord would be entitled to receive the entire insurance proceeds payable under any property insurance policies covering the Premises (or if Tenant self-insures, the amount that would have been payable under such policies), less any amount which is paid in connection with Tenant's trade fixtures or personal property which amount would be paid to (or retained by) Tenant. If Landlord does not elect to terminate this Lease then Tenant shall level the improvements, remove all debris and keep the Premises in good condition for the remainder of the Term, provided that Tenant shall be entitled to use any available insurance proceeds payable under any applicable property insurance policies covering the Premises to perform such work and the remainder of such proceeds (or if Tenant self-insures, the amount that would have been payable under such policies) following Tenant's completion of such work shall be paid to Landlord.

19. LIABILITY AND INDEMNIFICATION. Landlord shall not be liable to Tenant or Tenant's employees, agents, patrons or invitees, or any person whomsoever, for any injury to person or damage to property on or about the Premises (other than that caused by the gross negligence of Landlord or Landlord's employees or agents); and Tenant agrees to indemnify Landlord and hold it harmless from any loss, claim, damages, cost or expense suffered or incurred by Landlord by reason of any such damage or injury. Tenant shall not be liable to Landlord or Landlord's employees, agents, patrons or invitees, or any person whomsoever, for any injury to person or damage to property on or about the common areas of the Shopping Center outside of the Premises (other than that caused by the willful act or negligence of Tenant or Tenant's employees or agents); and Landlord agrees to indemnify Tenant and hold it harmless from any loss, claim, damages, cost or expense suffered or incurred by Tenant by reason of any such damage or injury.

20. CONDEMNATION. If, during the Term hereof, there is any taking of all or any part of the Premises by condemnation or by private purchase in lieu of condemnation, the rights and obligations of the parties shall be determined as follows:

Should all or such part of the Premises, be taken in such a manner as to interfere materially with Tenant's use and occupancy thereof or cause the Premises to fail to comply with any applicable Laws, then Tenant, by delivering written notice to the Landlord within thirty (30) days after such taking, may terminate this Lease, which date of termination shall be the actual date of taking. Landlord shall be entitled to any and all awards and payments made as a result of or on account of such taking except that Tenant shall be entitled to (i) the unamortized value of the then existing buildings and other improvements (based on straight line depreciation over the initial Term of this Lease) and (ii) those awards attributable to Tenant's equipment, goodwill and relocation expenses, provided such claims in clause (ii) do not diminish Landlord's award.

In the event of a partial taking of the Premises and this Lease is not canceled pursuant to the terms hereof, then this Lease shall terminate only as to the part so taken as of the date of the taking; and the Rental shall be equitably reduced. That portion of the Premises remaining after the taking shall thereafter be referred to as the "Premises". In the event of such partial taking, Landlord shall be entitled to any and all awards and payments, except Tenant may pursue a separate claim for its damages provided such claim does not diminish Landlord's award.

Neither Landlord nor Tenant shall be responsible or liable to the other for any taking and any award by settlement or litigation shall be the sole responsibility of the party claiming an interest in the property taken.

21. DEFAULTS BY TENANT; REMEDIES.

21.1 Defaults by Tenant. The occurrence of any one or more of the following events shall, upon the expiration of the applicable cure period, constitute a material default and breach of this Lease by Tenant:

(a) The failure by Tenant to make any payment of Rental or any other payment required to be made by Tenant hereunder as and when due within thirty (30) days after receipt of written notice from Landlord of such failure; or

(b) Tenant fails to pay any other sum or charge payable by Tenant hereunder as and when the same becomes due and payable, and such failure continues for more than 30 days after Landlord gives written notice of such failure to Tenant; or

(c) Tenant fails to perform or observe any other agreement, covenant, condition or provision of this Lease to be performed or observed by Tenant as and when performance or observance is due, and such failure continues for more than 30 days after Landlord gives written notice thereof to Tenant; or if the default cannot be cured within said 30 day period, Tenant fails within said 30 days to commence with due diligence and dispatch the curing of such default or, having so commenced, thereafter fails to prosecute or complete with due diligence and dispatch the curing of such default; or

(d) The making by Tenant of any general assignment for the benefit of creditors; the filing by or against Tenant of a petition to have Tenant adjudged a bankrupt or of a petition for reorganization or arrangement under any law relating to bankruptcy (unless in the case of a petition filed against Tenant, the same is dismissed within ninety (90) days); the appointment of a trustee or receiver to take possession of substantially all of Tenant's assets located in the Premises or of Tenant's interest in this Lease, where possession is not restored to Tenant within ninety (90) days; or the attachment, execution or other judicial seizure of substantially all of Tenant's assets located at the Premises or Tenant's interest in this Lease, where such seizure is not discharged within ninety (90) days; or

(e) The abandonment of the Premises by Tenant; provided, however, that Tenant's vacation of the Premises or its cessation of business in the Premises shall not be deemed to be an abandonment of the Premises as long as Tenant continues to perform its obligations under this Lease.

21.2 Remedies. In the event of any default or breach by Tenant as described above in this Section 21, Landlord may at any time thereafter, and without limiting Landlord in the exercise of any other right or remedy which Landlord may have by reason of such default or breach, exercise any one or more of the following remedies:

(a) Seek payment of all amounts due under this Lease, when due. If Tenant fails to pay any installment of rent or other sums on the due date and fails to cure such default within ten (10) days, the Tenant shall pay a charge equal to five percent (5 percent) of such installment as additional rent and as compensation to Landlord and not as a penalty. Unpaid installments of rent or other sums shall bear interest from the tenth (10th) day after the date due until paid at the lower of (i) the highest lawful contract rate or (ii) ten percent (10 percent) per annum (the "Default Rate").

(b) Terminate Tenant's right to possession of the Premises by any lawful means, with or without terminating the Lease, and Tenant shall immediately surrender possession of the Premises to Landlord. If Landlord elects this remedy Tenant shall remain liable for all amounts due pursuant to the terms of this Lease through the date the Lease is terminated in writing by Landlord.

(c) Maintain Tenant's right to possession, in which case this Lease shall continue in effect and Landlord shall be entitled to enforce all of Landlord's rights and remedies under this Lease, including the right to recover the Minimum Rental as it becomes due hereunder.

(d) Pursue any other remedy now or hereafter permitted or available to Landlord under the laws or judicial decisions of the Commonwealth of Virginia.

(e) Cure the default of Tenant itself; provided that if Landlord, by reason of Tenant's default, pays any sum or does any act that requires the payment of any sum, the sum paid by Landlord shall be immediately due from Tenant to Landlord upon payment and shall bear interest at the Default Rate from the date the sum is paid by Landlord until Landlord is reimbursed by Tenant. All such sums paid by Landlord together with interest thereon shall be additional rent hereunder.

Landlord's pursuit of any one remedy specified above shall not preclude its subsequent pursuit of any other available remedy. Failure to enforce one or more of the remedies herein provided upon a default shall not be deemed to constitute a waiver of such default or of any other violation or breach of this Lease.

22. DEFAULT BY LANDLORD. Landlord shall perform all conditions and covenants required to be performed by Landlord, as set forth in this Lease, including, but not limited to, making all payments required by Landlord to be made on any obligation secured by the real property subject to this Lease. Notwithstanding anything herein to the contrary,

Landlord shall not be deemed to be in default under this Lease unless and until Tenant has given written notice to Landlord (and, if requested by Landlord, to Landlord's mortgagee if the mortgagee has notified Tenant in writing of its interest and the address to which such notices are to be sent) of any such default by Landlord and Landlord has failed to cure such default within thirty (30) days after Landlord received notice thereof. Provided, however, that if the nature of Landlord's default is such that more than thirty (30) days are reasonably required for a cure, then Landlord shall not be deemed to be in default if Landlord commences such cure within the thirty (30) day period and thereafter diligently prosecutes the cure to completion. In the event Landlord should be in default of any obligation as herein set forth in this Section 22, or in any other manner under this Lease, and the applicable cure period has expired, Tenant shall be entitled to cure the default, at Tenant's option, including the payment of monies directly to the party to whom the obligation is owed, or Tenant may pursue any other remedy now or hereafter permitted or available to Tenant under the laws or judicial decisions of the Commonwealth of Virginia. Tenant shall be entitled to a fair and reasonable abatement of Rental during the time and to the extent that the Premises are untenantable as a result of Landlord's failure to perform any condition or covenant required by this Lease to be performed by Landlord.

23. LANDLORD'S ENTRY ON PREMISES. Landlord or its authorized representative shall, following reasonable prior notice to Tenant, have the right to enter the Premises at all reasonable times for any of the following purposes:

(a) To determine whether the Premises are in good condition and whether Tenant is complying with its obligations under this Lease;

(b) To serve, post or keep posted any notice as required or allowed under provisions of this Lease; and

(c) To do or perform or cause to be done or performed any act necessary for the safety or preservation of the Premises or the other improvements on the Premises (and be reimbursed by Tenant for all costs incurred thereby), provided that Landlord first notifies Tenant of the required curative or preventative work, and Tenant fails to complete such work within a reasonable period of time.

Landlord shall conduct its activities on the Premises as allowed in this Section 23 in a manner that will cause the least possible inconvenience, annoyance, or disturbance to Tenant. Landlord agrees to indemnify and hold Tenant harmless from and against any loss, liability or damage that the Tenant suffers which results from the negligence or willful act of Landlord, or its employees, agents or representatives.

24. NON-DISTURBANCE; SUBORDINATION. (a) Existing Rights, Liens or Leases. Landlord represents and warrants to Tenant that as of the Commencement Date neither the Premises nor this Lease shall be subject or subordinate to any lease (including any ground lease) or any other right held by any third party (e.g., option to purchase or lease, whether recorded or not), except as may be disclosed in writing to Tenant prior to the execution of this Lease by Tenant and Landlord. If, as of the full execution of this Lease, the Land is or will be subject to any lien in favor of any lender ("Lender"), then Landlord shall cause Lender to provide Tenant with an executed non-disturbance agreement in form and substance reasonably acceptable to Lender and Tenant.

(b) Subordination of Future Liens. Upon request of Landlord, Tenant will in writing, within fifteen (15) business days after the request, subordinate its rights under this Lease to any future mortgages or lien or any future deeds of trust to any bank, insurance company or other lending institution ("Future Lender"), hereafter in force against the Premises, Building or other improvements on the Premises, and upon any improvements hereafter placed upon the Land of which the Premises are a part, and to all advances made or hereafter to be made upon the security thereof; provided, however, that as a condition to such subordination, Landlord shall obtain an agreement from any and all Future Lenders that shall include a non-disturbance agreement which shall be executed by the party to whose interest Tenant subordinates its interest hereunder and shall meet the following requirements: (i) it shall provide that so long as Tenant is not in default under this Lease (beyond the applicable cure or grace period provided in the Lease), Tenant's leasehold estate, and Tenant's rights under this Lease including but not limited to possession, occupancy and use of the Premises in accordance with this Lease, shall remain undisturbed and shall survive any foreclosure, transfer in lieu of foreclosure or other enforcement of the mortgage or deed of trust, and any termination of any such lien, as the case may be; (ii) there shall be no change in the terms of this Lease, no diminution of Tenant's rights provided for in this Lease, and no additional liability of Tenant; and (iii) the documentation shall be otherwise satisfactory to Tenant in the exercise of its reasonable judgment.

25. WAIVER OF LANDLORD'S LIENS. Landlord hereby waives any lien for any rent it has against the Tenant or Tenant's property in the Premises, except for any judgment lien that may hereafter arise in favor of Landlord.

26. MECHANICS' LIEN. At all times during the Term of this Lease, Tenant shall keep the Premises free and clear of liens for labor, services, materials, supplies or equipment performed on or furnished to the Premises at the direction or order of Tenant and shall indemnify, defend and hold harmless Landlord (including, without limitation, for Landlord's attorneys' fees) against all liens and claims of liens for labor, services, materials, supplies, or equipment performed on or furnished to the Premises at the direction or order of Tenant. Tenant may contest any claim, charge or lien (including but not limited to mechanics' and materialmen's liens) and such contest on the part of Tenant and any failure to pay or perform the matter under contest, shall not be or become a breach or default under this Lease so long as the contest is conducted diligently, in compliance with applicable law, and by proceedings sufficient to prevent enforcement of the matter under contest and Tenant shall pay any amount adjudged by a court of competent jurisdiction to be due, with all costs, interest and penalties thereon, before the judgment becomes subject to execution against the Premises.

27. SURRENDER OF PREMISES. On expiration of the Term hereof or earlier termination pursuant to the terms hereof, Tenant shall surrender to Landlord the Premises and such improvements and alterations as have become part of the Premises pursuant to the terms hereof in good condition and repair, ordinary wear and tear excepted. Such fixtures, furnishings, equipment or alterations which Tenant has a right to remove or its obligated to remove under the provisions hereof shall be removed and repairs made for damages caused to the Premises not later than thirty (30) days following the expiration or termination of this Lease. Tenant shall surrender the Premises without any material damage to the Premises (ordinary wear and tear and damage by casualty and condemnation excepted) occasioned by the removal of Tenant's trade fixtures, furnishings and equipment and Tenant shall be responsible for any repairs required as a result of such damage. All furnishings, fixtures and

equipment used in the improvements and on the Premises and supplied and installed at the cost and expense of Tenant at all times shall be the sole property of Tenant.

The above and foregoing notwithstanding, no computer servers, desktop stations, laptops, files or other personal property which could reasonably be expected to contain customer information (collectively, the "Protected Items") shall become the property of or shall be disposed of by Landlord, but Landlord may arrange for storage of same at Tenant's cost for a period of not less than ninety (90) days, only after first providing an additional written notice to Tenant and five (5) additional business days, and access during Landlord's normal business hours, for Tenant to retrieve said items; it being acknowledged by both Landlord and Tenant that such items may contain sensitive, confidential and/or proprietary information which is subject to federal regulations as to ownership, possession, storage, disposal, removal or other handling. During any such period, not to exceed thirty-five (35) business days, that any Protected Items shall remain in the Premises, Tenant shall, in addition to ownership of such items, retain the right of possession and control of the Premises and Tenant shall pay therefore, Rental at the applicable holdover rate(s) established by this Lease for such additional time period.

If Tenant, with Landlord's consent, remains in possession of the Premises after the expiration of the Term hereof, such possession by Tenant shall be deemed to be a month-to-month tenancy, terminable on thirty (30) days notice given at any time by either party and Tenant shall pay as monthly Rental one hundred fifty percent (150 percent) of the monthly Rental payable during the prior month. All other provisions of this Lease except those pertaining to the term shall apply to this month-to-month holdover tenancy.

28. TIME OF ESSENCE. Time is of the essence with respect to each and every provision of this Lease. However, if the final date of any period which is set out in any provision of this Lease falls on a Saturday, Sunday or legal holiday under the laws of the United States or the Commonwealth of Virginia in such event, the time of such period shall be extended to the next day which is not a Saturday, Sunday or legal holiday.

29. INTERPRETATION OF LEASE; VENUE. This Lease shall be construed and interpreted in accordance with the laws of the Commonwealth of Virginia. Venue for any action regarding this Lease shall be Spotsylvania County, Virginia.

30. BINDING EFFECT. This Lease shall be binding upon the parties hereto, and their heirs, administrators, successors and assigns, where applicable.

31. INTEGRATION. This Lease and the documents specifically referred to herein, upon acceptance by the parties hereto, constitutes the sole and only agreement between Landlord and Tenant as to the subject matter hereof, and is intended by each to constitute the final written memorandum of all of their agreements and understandings in this transaction. No representations or warranties, express or implied, and no promises or prior agreements whatsoever have been made, agreed to, or entered into by Landlord or Tenant which are not expressly set forth herein; and if Landlord or Tenant has attempted to make such representations, warranties, promises or prior agreements, the same are each superseded hereby and waived.

32. ATTORNEYS' FEES. If any legal action or other proceeding is brought for the enforcement of this Lease, or because of an alleged dispute, breach or default, under this

Lease, or to interpret this Lease or any of the provisions hereof, the successful or prevailing party shall be entitled to recover reasonable attorneys' fees and other costs incurred in that action or proceeding whether or not the action or proceeding goes to final judgment, in addition to any other relief which it or they may be entitled to.

33. COUNTERPARTS. This Lease may be executed in any number of counterparts with the same force and effect as if all signatures were appended to one document, each of which shall be deemed an original.

34. INVALIDITY. If any term or provision of this Lease or application thereof is held invalid or unenforceable as to any party, the balance of the Lease shall not be affected thereby, and each remaining term and provision of this Lease shall be valid and shall be enforced to the fullest extent permitted by law.

35. NOTICE. Except as otherwise provided herein, any notice to be given hereunder by either party to the other shall be in writing and shall be deemed to be delivered upon the earlier of (i) when actually received at the office of the respective party, i.e., whether by delivery, mail or telecopy ("fax"), i.e., with a "fax" delivery being deemed to have been received on the date shown on the sender's confirmation copy, or (ii) whether actually received or not, on the first business day after it has been deposited with a nationally recognized overnight mail courier service, or (iii) whether actually received or not, three (3) business days after it has been deposited in the United States mail, postage fully prepaid, registered or certified mail, addressed to the intended recipient at the primary address stated below in this Section (or, if a change of address has been designated by the immediately succeeding sentence, then to the primary address specified in such notice), it being agreed that notices to a party's designated copy recipient(s) are to be undertaken but are not required for a notice to the party to be valid. Notices shall be addressed as set forth below, but each party can change its address by written notice to the other in accordance with this Section 36:

IF TO LANDLORD:

600 Dayton Lane
Fairfax, VA 00000
Attn: C. Jonathon Richards, Jr.
Telephone: 000-000-0000
Facsimile: 000-000-0000

With a copy to:

James E. Wilson, Jr.
Chief Financial Officer
600 Dayton Lane
Fairfax, VA 00000

IF TO TENANT:

America's Bank, N.A.
Attn. Joan – 5th floor

Mail Code: NC2-109-06-05
4444 Ivory Corp. Place
Charlotte, NC 28277

with a copy to: America's Bank, N.A.

Mail Code: MA5-503-06-01
Dallas Operations Center
725 Dawn Street, N.W.
Dallas, TX 00000
Attn: Shannon P. Muller

36.	NON-WAIVER. Any waiver or breach of the covenants herein contained to be kept and performed by either party hereto shall not be deemed or considered as a continuing waiver and shall not operate to bar or prevent the other party hereto from declaring a forfeiture, termination, or cancellation for any succeeding breach either of the same condition or covenant or otherwise. Acceptance of any payment required hereunder shall not be deemed a waiver.

37.	MISCELLANEOUS. The agreements contained herein shall not be construed in favor of or against either party, but shall be construed as if all parties prepared this Lease. Masculine and neuter genders, the singular number and the present tense, shall be deemed to include the feminine gender, plural number and past and future tenses, respectively, where the context so requires. The paragraph or section headings herein are used only for the purposes of convenience and shall not be deemed to limit the subject of the paragraphs or sections hereof.

38.	RIGHT TO ESTOPPEL CERTIFICATES. Each party, within fifteen (15) business days after notice from the other party, shall execute and deliver to the other party a certificate stating that this Lease is unmodified and in full force and effect, or in full force and effect as modified and stating the modifications and specifying the existence or absence of any default hereunder. This certificate shall also state the amount of Rental, the dates to which the Rental has been paid in advance, and the amount of any security deposit or prepaid Rental.

39.	RECORDING SHORT FORM OF LEASE. This Lease shall not be recorded but the parties hereto agree that they will execute, acknowledge, and deliver a short form of lease ("Short Form") to the end that the same may be recorded in the official records for the County in which the Premises are located. The parties further agree that the Short Form shall expressly include, without limitation, a description of the Premises, the Lease Term (including any renewal rights), any purchase options, rights of first offer or refusal, exclusive use rights or any other material rights granted Tenant under this Lease. Recording charges and any stamp or like tax shall be paid by Tenant.

40.	TITLE TO PREMISES; QUIET ENJOYMENT. Landlord represents and warrants to Tenant that Landlord has full legal right, authority and sufficient title to enter into this Lease. Upon Tenant paying the Rental reserved hereunder and observing and performing all of the covenants, conditions and provisions on Tenant's part to be observed and performed hereunder, Tenant shall have quiet possession of the Premises for the entire Term of this

Lease against the lawful act of any person or persons claiming by, through or under Landlord, subject to matters of public record.

41.   COMMISSION. In connection with this Lease, (1) Landlord has been represented by American Brokerage ("Landlord's Broker") and (2) Tenant has been represented by the Virginia Brokerage Company ("Tenant's Broker"). Landlord's Broker and Tenant's Broker are collectively referred to as "the Brokers." Landlord shall pay a commission ("Commission") to the Brokers in accordance with the terms of a separate agreement. Landlord represents and warrants to Tenant, and Tenant represents and warrants to Landlord that, except for the commission payable by Landlord to the Brokers, neither party has incurred any liability, contingent or otherwise, for brokerage or finder's fee or agent's commissions or other like payments in connection with this Lease, or the transactions contemplated hereby; and each party hereby agrees to hold harmless and indemnify the other from any claims, demands, causes of action or damages resulting from a breach of such representation and warranty.

42.   FORCE MAJEURE. Neither party shall be liable for any delay or failure to perform its non-monetary obligations hereunder due to (and the time for performance of any covenant shall be deemed extended by the time last due to) any causes beyond its reasonable control, including, without limitation, fire, accident, act of the public enemy, war, rebellion, insurrection, sabotage, transportation delay, labor dispute, shortages of material, labor, energy or machinery, or act of God, act of government or the judiciary.

43.   NO IMPLIED REPRESENTATIONS; "NET" LEASE. Except as may be expressly stated in this Lease, the Land is being leased by Landlord to Tenant in "AS IS, WHERE IS" condition, with all faults and deficiencies and with no implied representations or warranties by Landlord. In addition, Tenant agrees that except as may be expressly stated otherwise in this Lease, this Lease is a "net" lease, with Landlord having no responsibilities or obligations whatsoever.

44.   AUTHORITY. Tenant and Landlord each warrant and represent to the other that the person(s) signing this Lease on such party's behalf has authority to do so and to bind such party to the terms, covenants and conditions herein. Each shall deliver to the other promptly upon request all documents reasonably requested by the other evidencing such authority.

45. ENVIRONMENTAL MATTERS. (a) Definitions. (i) "Environmental Laws" shall mean all present and future statutes, ordinances, orders, rules and regulations of all federal, state or local governmental agencies relating to industrial hygiene, human health, environmental protection, or to the use, generation, manufacture, installation, release, discharge, storage, transportation or disposal of Hazardous Materials, including the Federal Water Pollution Act, as amended (33 U.S.C. section 1251 et seq.), the Resource Conservation and Recovery Act, as amended (42 U.S.C. section 6901 et seq.), the Comprehensive Environmental Response, Compensation and Liability Act of 1980, as amended (42 U.S.C. section 9601 et seq.), the Hazardous Materials Transportation Act, as amended (49 U.S.C. section 1801 et seq.), and/or comparable provisions of state and local laws; and (ii) "Hazardous Materials" shall mean Petroleum, asbestos, polychlorinated biphenyls, formaldehyde, radioactive materials, radon gas or any chemical, material or substance now or hereafter defined as or included in the definition of "hazardous substances", "hazardous wastes", "hazardous materials", "extremely hazardous waste", "restricted hazardous waste" or "toxic substances", or words of similar import, under any Environmental Laws.

158

(b) Warranty Regarding Hazardous Materials. Landlord warrants and represents to Tenant that, except for Hazardous Materials present within the Shopping Center as part of Landlord's business operation conducted in the ordinary course as part of a first-class shopping center in accordance with the standards of this Lease and in accordance with all Environmental Laws, Landlord has no actual knowledge of any Hazardous Materials located in, about, under, or upon the Shopping Center as of the date of this Lease. Landlord will disclose to Tenant information regarding the presence of any Hazardous Materials located in, on or about the Premises, or any adjacent common areas, parking areas and landscaping. Prior to Landlord's delivery of possession of the Premises to Tenant, Landlord, at its sole cost and expense will remove from the Premises any Hazardous Materials which are not permitted to be maintained on such property by applicable Environmental Laws.

(c) Use of Hazardous Materials. Neither party will handle, store, use or transport, or allow handling, storage, use, or transport of, Hazardous Materials on, about, under or in the Shopping Center, except as part of its business operation conducted in the ordinary course as part of a first-class shopping center in accordance with the standards of this Lease and in accordance with all Environmental Laws. Landlord shall have sole responsibility for the removal and/or remediation of any Hazardous Materials to the extent required by government authorities, in compliance with all Environmental Laws, discovered in, on or about the Premises and/or the Shopping Center, regardless of the date of its discovery, unless such Hazardous Materials were placed on the Premises and/or the Shopping Center by Tenant, or its agents, employees, invitees or contractors. If Hazardous Materials were placed on the Premises and/or the Shopping Center by Tenant, or its agents, employees, invitees or contractors, then Tenant shall have sole responsibility for the removal and/or remediation of any Hazardous Materials to the extent required by government authorities, in compliance with all Environmental Laws. In the event of a release in, about, under or on the Shopping Center, or any portion thereof, of any Hazardous Materials, the responsible party shall take the remedial actions necessary to clean up the release in accordance with Environmental Laws if and to the extent required by government authorities. Each party immediately will notify the other in writing of: (a) any enforcement, cleanup, removal or other governmental or regulatory action instituted, completed or threatened pursuant to any Environmental Laws; (b) any claim made or threatened by any person against Tenant, Landlord or the Premises relating to damage, contribution, cost recovery compensation, loss or injury resulting from or claimed to result from any Hazardous Materials; and (c) any reports made to any environmental agency arising out of or in connection with any Hazardous Materials in or removed from the Premises or the Shopping Center, including any complaints, notices, warnings or asserted violations in connection therewith. Each party also will supply to the other as promptly as possible, and in any event within 5 business days after the first party receives or sends the same, with copies of all claims, reports, complaints, notices, warnings or asserted, violations, relating in any way to the Premises or Tenant's use thereof.

(d) Indemnification. Tenant will indemnify, defend by counsel reasonably acceptable to Landlord, protect, and hold Landlord and each of Landlord's partners, employees, agents, attorneys, successors and assigns, free and harmless from and against any and all claims, liabilities, penalties, forfeitures, losses or expenses, including attorney's fees, for any death of or injury to any person or damage to any property whatsoever arising from or caused in whole or in part, directly or indirectly, by (a) the presence in, on, under or about the Premises caused by a discharge in or from the Premises of any Hazardous Materials placed in, under or about, the Premises by Tenant or any of Tenant's employees, agents, invitees or contractors; or (b) Tenant's use, analysis, storage, transportation, disposal, release, threatened release, discharge or generation of Hazardous Materials to, in, on, under, about or from the Premises; or (c) Tenant's failure to comply with any Hazardous Materials Law. Landlord will indemnify, defend by counsel reasonably acceptable to Tenant, protect, and hold Tenant and each of Tenant's employees, agents, attorneys, successors and assigns, free and harmless from and against any and all claims, liabilities penalties, forfeitures, losses or expenses, including attorney's fees, for death of or injury to any person or damage to any property whatsoever, arising from or caused in whole or in part, directly or indirectly, by the presence in, on, under or discharge in or from the Premises (or any other portion of the Shopping Center other than the Premises) of any Hazardous Materials placed in, on, under or about the Premises by Landlord or by any of Landlord's employees, agents or contractors, or (y) Landlord's use, analysis, storage, transportation, disposal, release, threatened release, discharge or generation of Hazardous Materials to, in, on, under, about or from the Premises; or (z) Landlord's failure to comply with any Hazardous Materials Law. The obligations of each party ("Indemnifying Party") pursuant to this Section includes, without limitation, and whether foreseeable or unforeseeable, all costs of any required or necessary repair, cleanup or detoxification or decontamination of the Premises, and the preparation and implementation of any closure, remedial action or other required plans in connection therewith, and survives the expiration or earlier termination of the Term of the Lease.

(e) Tenant's Work. In the event that Tenant encounters any Hazardous Materials on the Land placed in, on, under or about the Land by Landlord or by any of Landlord's employees, agents or contractors at any time during Tenant's Work as provided at Section 4.3, Tenant shall promptly notify Landlord of such fact, and Landlord shall promptly undertake abatement or remediation in accordance with all applicable laws, regulations and ordinances, and Tenant shall be entitled to a one-day tolling of any of its obligations pursuant to this Lease, including without limitation, its obligation to pay Rental, for each day Tenant is unable to proceed with Tenant's Work until such time as Landlord has caused such Hazardous Materials to be so abated or remediated.

1.   NO RELOCATION. Landlord shall not have the right to relocate Tenant from the Premises to any other space in the Shopping Center.

2.   WAIVER OF RIGHT TO JURY TRIAL. Landlord and Tenant hereby knowingly, voluntarily and intentionally waive the right to a trial by jury in respect of any litigation based hereon, arising out of, under or in connection with this Lease or any documents contemplated to be executed in connection herewith or any course of conduct, course of dealings, statements (whether oral or written) or actions of either party arising out of or related in any manner with the Premises (including without limitation, any action to rescind or cancel this Lease or any claims or defenses asserting that this Lease was fraudulently induced or is otherwise void or voidable). This waiver is a material inducement for Landlord and Tenant to enter and accept this Lease.

48.   RIGHT OF FIRST OPPORTUNITY. Landlord hereby grants to Tenant, under (and only under) the terms hereof, the right to purchase the Premises during the Term of this Lease. Except as set forth in the last sentence of this Section 48, Landlord shall give Tenant the right to purchase the Premises as set forth in this Section 48 prior to selling the Premises during the Term of this Lease. Landlord shall have the right at any time during the Term, to notify Tenant of a proposed sales price, which proposed sales price shall be a good faith proposal substantially equivalent to the price Landlord would present to any other

160

prospective purchaser of the Premises at the time the proposal is made. If Tenant accepts such proposed price within thirty (30) days, the parties shall close the sale of the Premises at such price. If Tenant does not accept such price within such thirty (30) days, then Landlord shall have the right, at any time during the Term, to sell and settle on the Premises at any price free of Tenant's right of first opportunity. Such first opportunity right shall be cancelled and terminated upon Tenant's failure to accept the proposed price as aforesaid.

In the event that Tenant shall exercise its right to purchase the Premises, Landlord covenants and agrees within thirty (30) days thereafter, upon payment of the purchase price agreed upon, to convey or assign, or cause to be conveyed or assigned, the Premises to Tenant, its successors and assigns, in fee simple, through a good and marketable title, subject to matters of record and by a special warranty deed. Taxes, water charges and other current expenses and rent hereunder shall be prorated as of the date of settlement. It is understood and agreed that in the event the title of Landlord be such as will not be guaranteed by any recognized title guaranty company, at such company's regular rates, Tenant may reject title to said property and cancel the exercise of the right to purchase. Intra-family transfers, transfers to entities in which Landlord is a substantial shareholder, transfers for estate or tax planning purposes, transfers incidental to the exercise of any remedy provided for in any deed of trust or mortgage encumbering the Land or the Premises, transfers to an Affiliate of Landlord and transfers of a larger parcel or multiple parcels including the Premises, are all exempt from the provisions of this Section, as are transfers after the expiration or earlier termination of this Lease.

49. RELEASE. At the termination of this Lease, if requested by Landlord, Tenant shall execute and deliver to Landlord an appropriate termination, in form proper for recording, of all Tenant's interest in the Premises, and upon request of Tenant, Landlord will execute and deliver a written cancellation and termination of Lease in proper form for recording; provided, that in no event shall any such cancellation or termination constitute a release or relinquishment by either party of its rights against the other party for any amounts payable by such other party under the terms of this Lease or any damages to which such party is entitled as a result of any default by the other party hereunder.

50. EXCULPATION. Notwithstanding anything contained in this Lease to the contrary, if at any time Landlord shall fail to perform or pay any covenant or obligation on its part to be performed or paid hereunder, and as a consequence thereof Tenant or its successors and assigns shall recover a money judgment against Landlord, such judgment shall (subject to the rights of any mortgagee or deed of trust holder whose lien predates the perfection of such judgment) be enforced against and satisfied out of only the proceeds of insurance, rent monies, condemnation, casualty or a sale produced upon execution of such judgment and levy thereon against Landlord's interest in the Premises and the improvements thereon and the Tenant and any other owner or holder of any claim or action against Landlord, shall look solely to the Premises and improvements thereon for the payment and satisfaction of any such claim or action and any judgment thereon. Furthermore, none of the agents or employees of the Landlord shall have any liability whatsoever for the performance or payment of any covenant or obligation of Landlord hereunder or upon any judgment thereon, all such liability hereby being expressly waived and released by the Tenant, its successors and assigns. Tenant shall not seek specific performance of any covenant or obligation by or against Landlord, except to the extent that the same can be enforced against the Premises and improvements thereon. The provisions of this Section are not intended to relieve Landlord from the performance of any of its obligations hereunder, but rather to limit Landlord's liability as aforesaid, and to relieve and release the agents and employees of the

Landlord from any such liability whatsoever, as aforesaid; nor shall any of the provisions of this Section be deemed to limit or otherwise affect Tenant's other rights specifically granted to the Tenant in this Lease. The provisions of this Section also shall inure to the benefit of Landlord's successors and assigns.

51. MODIFICATION. This Lease may be modified only by a written agreement signed by Landlord and Tenant.

52. NO JOINT VENTURE. The relationship between Landlord and Tenant shall at all times remain solely that of landlord and tenant and shall not be deemed a partnership or joint venture.

IN WITNESS WHEREOF, this Lease has been executed by the parties hereto as of the later of the dates accompanying a signature by Landlord and Tenant below.

LANDLORD: JOHNSON HOLDINGS, LLC, a Virginia limited liability company

By: NT PARTNERS, LLC, a Virginia limited liability company

By: _____

C. Jonathon Richards, Jr., President

Date of Landlord's Signature: _____, 2007

TENANT: AMERICA'S BANK, N.A., a national banking association

By: _____ John Harmon, Senior Vice President

Date of Tenant's Signature: _____, 2007

EXHIBIT "A"

LEGAL DESCRIPTION

Legal Description of the Premises

[TO BE ADDED ON RECEIPT OF THE TITLE COMMITMENT AND REVISED IN ACCORDANCE WITH THE SURVEY]

EXHIBIT "A-1"

SITE PLAN

[TO BE ADDED ON RECEIPT OF THE SITE PLAN AS MAY BE REVISED IN ACCORDANCE WITH THE SURVEY]

EXHIBIT "B"

CONSTRUCTION AGREEMENT

This Construction Agreement is attached to and made a part of the Lease to which it is attached. Any capitalized terms used but not defined in this Construction Agreement shall have the same meanings given such terms in the Lease.

1. Landlord's Work

1.1 Landlord, at Landlord's expense, shall be responsible for performing the following ("Landlord's Work"):

(a) grading of the Premises to 90 percent compaction +/- 6 inches to design grade of the building pad in accordance with the soils report prepared by Tenant which has been approved by Tenant (the "Soils Report"), with the balance of the Land to be graded for proper drainage.

(b) installation of water and sewer, stubbed to a point within five feet outside the property line for the Land (the "Property Line") as shown on the Site Plan.

(c) construction of all improvements which are required by government authorities as a condition to issuing building permits and/or a certificate of occupancy for the Building which are to be located outside the Premises (i.e., "off-site" improvements; including, without limitation, public street improvements or improvements adjacent thereto, driveways, de-acceleration lanes, median breaks, granting of easements, street lighting, utilities, traffic lights and controls, directional signage, fire hydrants, sewer line and storm drain improvements, retention area improvements, bus shelters and such other improvements associated with the development of the Shopping Center as shown on the Site Plan; provided, however, installation and/or construction of storm water drainage and or detention shall be the responsibility of Tenant.

1.2 Landlord shall perform all of Landlord's Work in a good and workmanlike manner and in compliance with all applicable laws, ordinances, building codes, regulations and other requirements (collectively, "Laws") including, without limitation, all requirements of the Americans with Disabilities Act and state and local disabled access laws (collectively, "ADA").

1.3 Following completion of the grading provided in Section 1.1(a) above, Landlord shall obtain and deliver to Tenant certification from the grading contractor in which such contractor certifies that it has performed all grading in accordance with the Soils Report and all Laws. In addition, Landlord shall assign to Tenant all warranties under the contract between Landlord and the grading contractor.

1.4 Landlord shall notify Tenant in writing when Landlord's Work has been completed in all material respects. Tenant shall within 30 days after the date of Landlord's notice inspect the

Premises and prepare a "punchlist" of work that is uncompleted and/or defective and deliver said list to Landlord. Landlord shall promptly cause all items on the punchlist to be completed or remedied. Landlord shall cause the performance of any remedial work required of the grading/earthwork within 15 days after written notice from Tenant.

1.5 Landlord shall cooperate with Tenant (at no cost or expense to Landlord) in connection with the installation and connection with all other utilities.

2. Tenant's Work. Tenant shall, at Tenant's sole cost and expense, perform all such work ("Tenant's Work") to construct, in compliance with all applicable laws, ordinances, building codes, regulations and other requirements (including the Building Standards for Harrison Road Shopping Center and the proffers contained in the Notice of Conditional Zoning) and in a good and workmanlike manner, the Building in accordance with the Approved Plans (as defined below) and the provisions of this Lease.

3. Approved Plans.

(a) Preliminary Plans. Tenant shall deliver the preliminary plans and specifications ("Preliminary Plans") for Tenant's Work to Landlord. Within 15 days following receipt of the Preliminary Plans, Landlord shall review the Preliminary Plans and shall deliver to Tenant its specific objections, if any, to the Preliminary Plans together with its proposed solution for each objection. Tenant shall thereafter, within 21 days revise and resubmit such revised Preliminary Plans to Landlord for review and approval. Subject to Section 3(b) below, this process shall be repeated until Landlord approves the Preliminary Plans.

(b) Right to Terminate. If the parties are unable to resolve Landlord's reasonable objections within forty-five (45) days after Tenant has received notice of the objections, Landlord or Tenant may, by written notice to the other party, terminate this Lease in which event this Lease shall automatically terminate and thereafter neither party shall have any further rights or obligations hereunder.

(c) Approved Plans. Once the Preliminary Plans have been approved, Tenant shall prepare and deliver to Landlord a set of final plans and specifications and working drawings ("Final Plans") based on the approved Preliminary Plans covering the construction of the Tenant's Work. Landlord and Tenant shall indicate their approval of the Final Plans and specifications and working drawings by initialing the same and thereafter they shall be deemed the "Approved Plans".

(d) Permits and Government Approvals. Tenant shall obtain approval of the Approved Plans and the necessary building permit(s) for construction of the Building on the Premises in accordance with the Approved Plans from all appropriate government agencies. Tenant shall exercise reasonable efforts and due diligence in attempting to obtain the Building Permit and all other necessary governmental approvals as soon as possible, in accordance with Section 5(e) of the Lease.

1.   Landlord's Right to Enter. During the course of construction, Landlord or its representatives may enter upon the building site at all reasonable times for the purpose of inspecting the construction to determine that the work is being completed in accordance with the Approved Plans and in compliance with all Laws. In no event shall such entry by Landlord interfere with the completion of Tenant's Work.

164

2.	Tenant's Construction Obligations. Tenant agrees that Tenant's Work shall be performed in accordance with the Approved Plans and in compliance with all Laws, in a good and workmanlike manner. If Landlord shall notify Tenant in writing of any defect in construction, Tenant shall within ten (10) days thereafter commence a cure of such defect and complete such cure with diligence at Tenant's sole cost and expense.

6.	Easements for Storm Water Drainage. In the event it is necessary or advisable that installation and/or construction of storm water drainage and detention by Tenant be performed over or within portions of land located outside the Premises, Landlord agrees to execute upon request by Tenant any and all easement as may be required by City, State or Federal governing agencies, or by any utility company in connection with the construction of storm water drainage and detention service to the Premises by Tenant, but only if and to the extent agreed upon by Landlord and Tenant which agreement Landlord shall not unreasonably withhold, condition or delay.

7. Timing of Construction and Rent Commencement Date.

(a) Delay of Rent Commencement Date. The Rent Commencement Date shall be delayed by one (1) day for: each day of delay in the substantial completion of the design and construction of Tenant's Work and in the move into the Premises that is caused by any Force Majeure Delay or Landlord Delay (as defined below).

(b) Force Majeure Delay. The term "Force Majeure Delay" as used in this Construction Agreement shall mean any delay in the completion of Tenant's Work which is attributable to any: (1) actual delay or failure to perform attributable to any strike, lockout or other labor or industrial disturbance (whether or not on the part of the employees of either party hereto), civil disturbance, act of a public enemy, war, riot, sabotage, blockade, embargo, inability to secure customary materials, supplies or labor through ordinary sources by reason of regulation or order of any government or regulatory body; or (2) delay attributable to lightning, earthquake, fire, storm, hurricane, tornado, flood, washout, explosion, or any other similar industry-wide or city-wide cause beyond the reasonable control of the party from whom performance is required, or any of its contractors or other representatives. Any prevention, delay or stoppage due to any Force Majeure Delay shall excuse the performance of the party affected for a period of time equal to any such prevention, delay or stoppage.

(c) Landlord Delay. The term "Landlord Delay" as used in the Lease or this Agreement shall mean any delay in the completion of Tenant's Work which is due to any act or omission of Landlord (wrongful, negligent or otherwise), its agents or contractors (including acts or omissions while acting as agent or contractor for Tenant). The term Landlord Delay shall include, but shall not be limited to any: (1) delay in the giving of authorizations, approvals, or disapprovals by Landlord; or (2) delay attributable to the acts or failures to act, whether willful, negligent or otherwise, of Landlord, where such acts or failures to act delay the completion of Tenant's Work; or (3) delay attributable to the material interference of Landlord, its agents or contractors with the completion of Tenant's Work or the continuing or material failure or refusal of any such party, after the delivery of possession of the Premises to Tenant to permit Tenant, its agents or contractors, access to and use of the Shopping Center or any Shopping Center facilities or services, which access and use are required for the orderly and continuous performance of the work necessary to complete Tenant's Work. In no event shall Tenant's remedies or entitlements for the occurrence of a Landlord Delay be abated, deferred, diminished or rendered inoperative because of a prior, concurrent, or subsequent delay resulting from any action or inaction of Tenant.

1.   No Fee to Landlord or Miscellaneous Charges. Landlord shall receive from Tenant no fee for supervision, profit, overhead or general conditions in connection with Tenant's Work or the Landlord's Work. Neither the Tenant nor the Tenant's contractor shall be charged for, and Landlord shall provide, parking (to the extent parking is available) for Tenant's architects, designers, contractors and subcontractors (including those people working on Tenant's Work).

2.   Bonding. Notwithstanding anything to the contrary set forth in the Lease, Tenant shall not be required to obtain or provide any completion or performance bond in connection with any construction, alteration, or improvement work performed by or on behalf of Tenant.

3.   Signage. During the construction of Tenant's Work, subject to Landlord's reasonable approval, Tenant shall have the right to install signs stating to the effect "Bank of America coming soon."

EXHIBIT "C"

INTENTIONALLY OMITTED

EXHIBIT "D"

PROHIBITED USES

The following uses are not permitted in or on the Leased Premises:

1) Any use which emits an obnoxious odor, which can be smelled outside of the Leased Premises.

2) Any use which emits a noise or sound, which can be heard outside of the Leased Premises.

3) Any operation primarily used as a storage warehouse operation.

4) Any operation primarily used for assembly, manufacturing, distilling, refining or smelting.

5) Any pawn shop.

6) Any second-hand store except shops dealing with antiques, collectables or historical items.

7) Any surplus store, including any store whose primary purpose is the sale of insurance salvage stock. No outdoor sales of any kind without Seller's approval.

8) Any mobile home park or trailer court.

9) Any junkyard or stockyard.

10) Any church or religious center.

11) Any civic or social lodge.

12) Any drug rehab center.

13) Any refuge center.

14) Any abortion clinic or Planned Parenthood facility.

15) Any industrial warehouse.

16) Any fire sale, tent sale, disaster or liquidation sale, (except as permitted in connection with Tenant's bankruptcy).

17) Any central laundry.

18) Any commercial truck sales, leasing, display or repair. Any automobile, RV or other vehicle sales or repair facility, including tires, batteries or accessories.

19) Any animal raising facility.

20) Any mortuary, crematorium or funeral home.

21) Any massage parlor except licensed massage therapists.

22) Any adult (pornographic) book store, sex shop or any establishment selling or exhibiting pornographic materials or drug-related paraphernalia.

23) Any dumping or disposing of garbage.

24) Any incineration or reduction of garbage.

25) Any bar, unless part of a full-service restaurant.

26) Any manufacturer of explosives or gunpowder.

27) Any abattoir.

28) Any body repair shop.

29) Any use that is prohibited by any document of record.

Made in the USA
Charleston, SC
01 October 2010